A publication in

The NORC Series in Social Research

National Opinion Research Center

Norman M. Bradburn, Director

Crime and Punishment— Changing Attitudes in America

Arthur L. Stinchcombe
Rebecca Adams
Carol A. Heimer
Kim Lane Scheppele
Tom W. Smith
D. Garth Taylor

Crime and Punishment— Changing Attitudes in America

Jossey-Bass Publishers

San Francisco • Washington • London • 1980

CRIME AND PUNISHMENT–CHANGING ATTITUDES IN AMERICA
by Arthur L. Stinchcombe, Rebecca Adams, Carol A. Heimer, Kim
Lane Scheppele, Tom W. Smith, and D. Garth Taylor

Copyright © 1980 by: Jossey-Bass Inc., Publishers
433 California Street
San Francisco, California 94104

&

Jossey-Bass Limited
28 Banner Street
London EC1Y 8QE

Library of Congress Cataloging in Publication Data
Main entry under title:

Crime and punishment–changing attitudes in America.

(The NORC series in social research)
Bibliography: p. 162
Includes index.
1. Crime and criminals–United States–Public
opinion. 2. Punishment–United States–Public opinion.
3. Public opinion–United States. I. Stinchcombe,
Arthur L. II. Series: National Opinion Research
Center. NORC series in social research.
HV6791.C74   364'.973   80-8004
ISBN 0-87589-472-0

Manufactured in the United States of America

JACKET DESIGN BY WILLI BAUM

FIRST EDITION

Code 8036

The Jossey-Bass
Social and Behavioral Sciences Series

Preface

This book is directed to those who investigate public opinion, criminology, and social change. The Social Change Project at the National Opinion Research Center, funded by the National Science Foundation, is primarily designed to report on changes in public opinion. It has produced a large archive of repeated poll questions since 1948, a series of papers on routine methods for dredging in this mass to find social changes, and a series of reports on changes in public opinion in recent times.

A large flow of new facts of this kind creates a number of puzzles, and this book is about one group of puzzles we found. It reports on changes in public opinion about crime and punishment, and to some degree it tests theories and hypotheses as would a monograph on the theory of public opinion. But most of the simple theories one might derive from the literature on public opinion turn out not to be true. The relative dominance of reporting over theory is partly a result of the failure of theory and partly reflects our belief that theory has been considerably oversold as a method for advancing knowledge. We are not therefore dismayed that our work is of a "puzzle expanding" rather than a "theory testing" sort.

Perhaps the most fundamental puzzle that started us off is that punitive attitudes, favoring capital punishment and harsher courts, moved in the opposite direction over time from other "illiberal" attitudes. Being lenient with criminals is traditionally correlated with liberalism; less racist or more civil libertarian people, for example, are less harsh on criminals. But while public opinion has been getting more civil libertarian, more feminist, less racist, more sexually liberal, and more sup-. portive of abortion, it has been getting more punitive toward criminals. The obvious explanation seemed to be that crime and fear of crime were increasing (Chapman, 1976; Greenwood and Wadycki, 1975). But fear of crime does not correlate strongly with punitiveness, and there are massive exceptions to that correlation. Blacks and women, who are much more afraid of crime, are less punitive than whites or men.

During the various stages of development of this book, the Social Change Project was directed by James A. Davis, Arthur L. Stinchcombe, and D. Garth Taylor. Most of the writing and analysis was done while Stinchcombe directed the project.

The chapter authors took pieces of the puzzle and tried to make sense of bits of data in first drafts. The puzzle pieces were distributed as follows: Chapter One, Arthur L. Stinchcombe; Chapter Two, Tom W. Smith and Rebecca Adams; Chapter Three, Rebecca Adams and Carol A. Heimer; Chapter Four, Arthur L. Stinchcombe; Chapter Five, Tom W. Smith and Kim Lane Scheppele; Chapter Six, D. Garth Taylor; Chapter Seven, D. Garth Taylor and Arthur L. Stinchcombe. Allan McCutcheon, A. Wade Smith, and Mark Reiser also participated in the project and in the discussions of the chapters.

Stinchcombe prepared a first draft of the book from the chapter drafts. Details often appear in places not intended by the original authors, supporting arguments written by someone else. In this process, what were originally chapter drafts were often turned into chapter fragments distributed in several chapters—an occurrence which the original chapter authors view as economical but not at all satisfactory, as it renders their work means rather than ends.

With helpful criticism by James A. Davis, Ben Page, James Q. Wilson, Kenneth Prewitt, Frederic L. Dubow, David Seidman, Andrew Greeley, and others, three further drafts were prepared by various people. Chapter Six is based on the article "Salience of Crime and Support for Harsher Criminal Sanctions" (Taylor, Scheppele, and Stinchcombe, 1979) which grew out of this revision process; we thank the publisher of *Social Problems* for permission to use some of that material here.

A preface is supposed to express also the sentimental ties that held the enterprise together and that tied its participants to the world. We quite often hurt each other, got angry, and were ashamed when it turned out that we had been wrong. We were, in short, an ideal-typical work team. Our main difficulties were the conflict between scheduling our collective work and our individual professional lives and the lack of match between status, salary, and contribution. But, within reasonable limits, we still like and respect each other.

It seems to us that the principal purpose of institutions is to enable people in them to do what they think wise or desirable. The National Science Foundation, the National Opinion Research Center, and the Institute for Research on Poverty at the University of Wisconsin, Madison, can be counted successes on that ground. We thank them for their support.

Tucson, Arizona   ARTHUR L. STINCHCOMBE
August 1980

Contents

The Authors

ARTHUR L. STINCHCOMBE is professor of sociology at the University of Arizona. He received his A.B. degree in mathematics from Central Michigan College (1953) and a Ph.D. degree in sociology from the University of California at Berkeley (1960). Stinchcombe is a former professor of sociology at the University of Chicago and senior study director at the National Opinion Research Center. He is a member of the American Sociological Association.

Stinchcombe is currently working on research in historical methodology, quantitative methodology, social and cultural change, and deviant behavior. He is the author of numerous books and articles in these fields, including *Theoretical Methods in Social History* (1978), *Creating Efficient Industrial Administrations* (with R. Marder and Z. Blum, 1974), and *Constructing Social Theories* (1968).

REBECCA G. ADAMS is research associate at the Education Resource Center and research projects specialist at the Social

Psychiatry Study Center. She received her B.A. degree in sociology from Trinity College (Hartford, Connecticut) (1974) and her M.A. degree in sociology from the University of Chicago (1977); currently she is working on her doctoral dissertation. She belongs to the American Sociological Association, Sociologists for Women in Society, and Gerontological Society.

At the Education Resource Center, a community-based teacher's center in Chicago, Adams and her colleagues are conducting an organizational case study of the Center. She is also researching relationships between concurrent and developmental family characteristics and social and psychological outcomes; recently she has focused on the consequences of teenage motherhood.

CAROL A. HEIMER is an instructor in sociology at the University of Arizona. She received her B.A. degree in sociology from Reed College (1973), a M.A. degree in sociology from the University of Chicago (1976), and is a doctoral candidate in sociology at the University of Chicago. She is a member of the American Sociological Association and Sociologists for Women in Society, and has worked as a research assistant at the National Opinion Research Center.

Heimer is currently interested in the fields of social stratification, formal organizations, deviance and social control, and the sociology of risk or uncertainty. She has published articles and presented papers on various aspects of crime and on racial and sexual attitudes in America; her book reviews have appeared in the *American Journal of Sociology* and the *Newsletter* of the Midwest Sociologists for Women Society.

KIM LANE SCHEPPELE is assistant professor of sociology at Bucknell University and research associate at the Center for the Social Sciences, Columbia University. She received her A.B. degree in urban studies from Barnard College (1975) and her M.A. degree in sociology from the University of Chicago (1977), where she is completing her doctoral studies in sociology.

Her research in public opinion includes work on feminist attitudes of men and women. In keeping with her interests in crime and in the sociology of women, she has worked with Pauline Bart of the University of Illinois at Chicago Circle on a study of Chicago rape victims and rape avoiders. Scheppele's book reviews and articles have appeared in such journals as the *American Journal of Sociology, Social Problems,* and *Contemporary Sociology.*

TOM W. SMITH is associate study director of the General Social Survey at the National Opinion Research Center, University of Chicago. He received B.A. degrees in history and political science (1971) and the M.A. degree in history (1972) from Pennsylvania State University, and he received his Ph.D. degree in American history from the University of Chicago (1979). He is a member of the Organization of American Historians and the Midwest Association for Public Opinion Research.

Smith has written extensively in the field of social change and social indicators, including works on capital punishment in *Studies of Social Change Since 1948* (1976) and on gun control in the *Journal of Criminal Law and Criminology* (forthcoming). Smith is currently studying trends in the most important problem over the last thirty years and serving on a National Academy of Sciences panel on Survey-Based Measures of Subjective Phenomena.

D. GARTH TAYLOR is assistant professor in the Department of Political Science at the University of Chicago and senior study director at the National Opinion Research Center. He earned a B.A. degree in psychology from the University of California at Berkeley (1971) and a M.A. degree in social sciences (1973), and a Ph.D. degree in sociology, both from the University of Chicago (1978). He is a member of the Section on Survey Research Methods of the American Statistical Association and of the American Association for Public Opinion Research.

Taylor is currently working on studies of urban politics, crime, busing, and neighborhood change. He is also a principal investigator in the national consortium that is evaluating and redesigning the National Crime Survey, sponsored by the Law Enforcement Assistance Administration. He has written about American racial attitudes for *Scientific American, Annals of the American Academy of Political and Social Science,* and *School Desegregation: Past, Present, and Future* (forthcoming).

Crime and Punishment— Changing Attitudes in America

1

The Public as Victim of Crime

. . . .
. . . .
. . . .

Americans generally do not walk on dangerous streets at night, and this decreases their probability of being robbed. But they would rather live in a society in which one could stroll at night. They may concede that street lights are necessary for crime control, but they sometimes wish they could see the stars. Changing the lock whenever one misplaces a key is a realistic adaptation to the probabilities of burglary, but is one of many minor irritations resulting from crime.

Social science research has emphasized that victims often participate in the interaction that leads to crimes like assault, murder, and rape (Amir, 1971; Curtis, 1974; Hindelang, 1976; von Hentig, 1948; Wolfgang, 1958), but a battered face or death is a disproportionate punishment for the crime of insulting one's husband, and a society in which flirtation commits a woman to sexual intercourse is an unfair society. Victims often do contribute to the crimes in which they are victimized, but in a less violent society one does not risk one's life in every dispute or assault in every flirtation.

1

It is traditional in every major civilization that crime is treated as a problem that damages the well-being of the entire public. The public interest in crime reflects the common sense observations made above: the public is damaged if it cannot see the stars because of crime-preventing streetlights, if it cannot get angry without risking death, if it cannot flirt without making love.

The high violent crime rate in the United States affects the quality of life of people who are not directly victimized. We will present evidence that the public knows this and knows that crime creates public policy problems, as well as private problems of locks and staying in at night. The basic subject of this book is how the public reacts to high crime rates and what they think should be done to protect the public's interest in domestic tranquility.

Data on Crime and Punishment

Polls and surveys, for all their difficulties, provide the most useful data on public opinion. We have regular poll measures on how important the crime problem is since 1946, on fear of walking at night since 1965, on capital punishment attitudes since 1936, on whether courts are harsh enough since 1965, and on gun registration since 1959. Therefore, poll data on some elements of public reaction to crime are available before, during, and after the recent large increase in the rate of violent crime. This enables us to observe the effect of a change in the crime level on public opinion on crime and punishment.

However, when using time-series data, it is usually the case that too many things change at once for causal inferences to be solid. Although it is true that we have data from low-crime years and high-crime years on attitudes toward capital punishment, there were many other things that distinguished the late 1960s and early 1970s from earlier, low-crime years than simply increases in violent crime. For example, the later years were after the civil rights movement and the Vietnam war and their related protests; were generally characterized by higher per-capita income; had higher educational qualifications for many jobs and a higher youth unemployment rate, especially among poorly educated youth; and was a time of much greater public support for liberal positions on race relations, civil liberties, feminism, and abortion.

One advantage of well-designed surveys on crime is that they measure many features of the lives and attitudes of people along with their attitudes on crime. We can find out, for example, whether people who live nearer ghettoes are more punitive. (They are not.) We can also find out whether people who are more prejudiced against blacks are more punitive. (They are.) Then we can supplement differences between years with differences between people in various situations (for example, near or far from the ghetto) to determine whether people who are more afraid of crime *both* in recent years *and* near ghettos are more punitive. When we find that people are more punitive in recent years but not in more dangerous neighborhoods, we are confronted with a new problem; but we would not know we had this problem without several ways of measuring the effect of exposure to high crime rates—some over time and some between individuals at one point in time.

The advantage of supplementing time-series data with surveys measuring many variables is perhaps even clearer in the relation of prejudice to punitiveness. During recent years, the level of prejudice of the American white public has been declining while the level of punitiveness has been increasing, possibly leading to the inference that liberals on racial questions are becoming more punitive. However, in the cross-sectional survey, when we study differences between people, we find that liberalism leads to lower punitiveness. To avoid false inferences from the time series, then, we need a survey with measures of both prejudice and punitiveness.

The General Social Surveys (GSS), conducted by the National Opinion Research Center under the direction of James A. Davis and supported by the National Science Foundation, are ideally designed for establishing connections between time-series and cross-sectional analysis. Most of the questions are adopted word for word from previous polls, with the time series for many questions extending up to the present. These are not special-purpose surveys of crime, race prejudice, or occupational and family experience; rather, they are general surveys that measure many attitudinal, behavioral, and biographical variables of demonstrated importance or interest. Thus, polls going back in time, combined with General Social Surveys for recent times and for extensive cross-sectional analysis, provide a rich set of analytic possibilities. The specific subject of this book, then, is how the public reacts to high crime rates insofar as this can be studied by a series of polls over time combined with cross-sectional analysis of the General Social Surveys.

From a formal statistical point of view, our dependent variables in this book are the answers to various poll questions on fear, courts, capital punishment, and gun registration. We are interested in these variables because they describe how people think about crime and crime control and because they enable us to describe changes over time in the way people think about crime.

People have much more complex ideas about the causes and control of crime than is reflected in simple "favor" or "oppose" answers to a capital punishment question. Therefore, it may be useful to address the issue of *how* people think about the causes of crime and its control, so as to have more clearly in mind how our simple poll questions relate to the psychological reality we would like to capture. For this purpose we will adopt a scheme for the analysis of motive developed by Burke (1969). Burke argues that philosophical and literary accounts of the motives of actions can be grouped according to whether they emphasize one or another of the following list of elements of action: (1) the scene of action, (2) the agent who engages in the action, (3) the instruments of action, (4) the act itself, and (5) the purpose.

For example, a street robbery might be analyzed as follows: (1) What scenes provide the opportunity and motivating circumstances for the crime (such as dark nighttime streets of the ghetto where a well-dressed pedestrian walks alone)? (2) What kinds of people are most likely to commit violent crimes against strangers (desperately poor people, habitual criminals, unfortunate junkies, young men proving their manhood, decent boys exposed to bad company)? (3) What effect does the free availability of small concealable hand-guns have on the likelihood that the robber can make an effective threat to carry out the robbery? (4) What are the features of the act itself that allow the crime to come to a successful conclusion (for example, is resistance in a robbery more likely to foil the robbers or to result in death)? (5) What are the purposes of the robber, and would a universal practice of carrying only credit cards reduce the motivation for the crime?

Most ordinary people, if properly questioned, would be found to have more or less well-developed theories of each of these "crime-producing elements." They show they understand crime scenes by staying off ghetto streets at night. They show they understand criminal agents by wanting to imprison habitual criminals more than temporarily mixed-up boys. They show they understand the means of crime by endorsing (in very large majorities) gun control. They show they understand the development of the criminal acts by attempting to call policemen if they see a crime from their windows. They show they understand purposes of crime by having their Social Security checks deposited directly in the bank and by having bus and taxi drivers carry little or no change.

Because of the particular surveys we used, the poll questions studied in this book tap aspects of the potential scenes and instruments of crime. Our data base includes questions measuring fear of crime in one's neighborhood, public views on the potential costs and benefits of crime as determined by harsher punishments, and public views on gun control. Although many of the practical activities people take with respect to crime—such as locking doors or installing burglar alarms—are oriented toward interfering with the criminal act itself, we have no questions in that area. And even though popular criminology is replete with theories on what kinds of people commit crimes, we have no questions on what makes for a criminal character and what should be done about it.

In spite of the "thinness" of the data we are able to develop some complex theories. Much of the book argues that

a person's response to one of the questions is determined by
thoughts about some other aspect of the elements of crime
motivation. For example, we will find that owners of guns are
much more opposed to gun registration than nonowners. One
possible explanation is that gun owners know what kind of
people own guns, and they do not believe that by registering
people like themselves one can control crime. The gun lobby
frequently makes the argument of agent rather than agency—
"Guns don't kill people—people kill people." To cite another
example, much of the American white public has come to
differentiate between the ghetto and individual black people.
They believe ghettos have unsafe streets, undisciplined schools,
and trash on the lawns, while they know individual black
people who are law abiding, work hard in school, keep a clean
yard, and are appropriate for personal friendship. The reason we
examine opinions on black people as agents and the ghetto as
a scene is to explain why there is a weak relationship between
punitive attitudes toward criminals and ordinary race prejudice
but a very strong relation between punitiveness and opposition
to busing (Kelley, 1974).

The point is that our poll questions on attitudes toward
crime and punishment tap only a few aspects of the public's
overall views about the causes and control of crime. But the
relations between these questions and other attitudes show
patterns that may be explained by hypotheses about the complex cognitive and attitudinal structure that people bring to
bear in interpreting crime.

Attitudes and Ideologies About Crime

At various points in this book, we consider the relationship between people's complex cognitive structures on crime
and their general ideologies about social matters. For example,
the Enlightenment tradition is one of coherence among attitudes forming a "general liberalism" ideology—a structure of
attitudes that distinguishes liberals from conservatives on cultural and social matters. In Chapter Four we will consider the
relationship between general liberalism and punitiveness. We

will argue that general liberalism may cause people to focus on the impact of the scene ("Do slums cause crime?") rather than the agent ("Do bad people cause crime?") and may influence their perception of the trustworthiness of agents of the law ("Can courts be trusted to be fair to black people?"). In Chapter Six we will ask whether this general liberal ideology is more coherent in high-crime neighborhoods—whether, when confronted with crime, people are forced to think about the role of crime in general public policy.

The statistical form of these investigations is to ask how strongly the poll questions on crime correlate with other questions measuring general liberalism. We find there is some "constraint" on the attitude structure as a whole (Converse, 1964), so that it is hard to hold very liberal and very punitive views at the same time. (This constraint, however, is not strong enough to render punitive attitudes a mere offshoot of the general liberal tradition.) In contrast, we find that opposition to gun control can be regarded as a part of a frontier hunting culture, being found in families and ethnic groups who emerged in nineteenth-century rural America.

Questions on the coherence of ideologies cannot be studied by individual questions, no matter how well those questions tap cognitive contents on crime, because the objects of the questions are relations among attitudes and between attitudes and geographic, ethnic, and other measures of cultural traditions. This is an additional reason for depending heavily on cross-sectional analyses in studying the time trends; what we have to deal with is the fate over time of whole ideologies and cultures rather than of opinions on particular questions.

An Analysis of Burke's Elements of Action

The "scene" of crime combines two different elements: a *situation* and an *environment*—that are causally connected. For example, a woman's boyfriend stays home during the day with her teenage daughter while the mother works: this is a *situation* tending to cause sexual child abuse or rape. Family systems with unstable marriages, repetitive living together

without marriage, and illegitimate births early in the life of the
mother tend to increase the probability of such situations and
so constitute a predisposing *environment* for sexual child
abuse and rape.

We will show that people recognize variations in the
crime producing qualities of situations and environments, by
showing for example that people are more afraid of the streets
if they are older or female, if the streets are near a ghetto, or
if they live alone. It is possible for scholarly analyses to identify
a ghetto as a collection of situations that produce crime (for
example, by having statistically more boyfriends of mothers
home with teenage daughters), as a collection of people who are
more inclined toward crime (by being undereducated, unemployed youth), or as a structure in which criminal acts are less
likely to be interfered with (because residents do not trust the
police or because public policy does not invest adequate policing resources in poor neighborhoods). In expressing their
opinions on crime, members of the public also seem to make
these distinctions—although without a systematic division of
crime into five elements, with two components of "scene," and
so forth.

People think about the "agents" of crime in a bifurcated
way. They are well aware of the demography of violent crime—
that it tends to be committed by young men, especially poor or
black young men. But they also believe that there are specific
people of "bad character" among those groups who are much
more involved in crime than their peers. They may believe that
these "bad characters" are dope addicts, errant boys who will
later reform, the youthful unemployed, or simply "bad guys."
People are aware of general predispositional qualities of demo-
graphic groups leading to higher crime rates; very few will run
from a young woman on the street at night. But in their thinking about crime policy they also differentiate specifically
criminal from merely unfortunate members of those groups.

The distinctions the public makes in the area of instruments or agencies of crime are more ad hoc. People generally
know that pistols are used in crimes more often than rifles or
shotguns and that butcher knives are used in gang fights less

often than switchblades; they will worry about a son who buys a switchblade but will leave the butcher knives in the kitchen drawer. They know that generally crime is easier with specially designed instruments and that bolt cutters will defeat most bicycle chains. They favor laws against carrying concealed weapons, and they would like a policeman to investigate when they see a young man standing near a bike rack with bolt cutters.

People's ideas about the criminal acts themselves seem to be much more primitive, perhaps because a person may be expected to experience a violent crime only once every fifty years (see Chapter Two). Ideas about the sequence of actions in a crime thus are more likely to come from television than from actual experience. There is ample folk wisdom on how a victim should act during a crime—for example, "Don't risk your life for a hundred dollars in a robbery" or (the cynical male advice about rape) "Lie back and enjoy it." Perhaps the most developed area of advice relates to protecting a home or business against burglary: lights, locks, burglar alarms, fences around the yard, and other mechanical devices to make a burglary more difficult are frequently analyzed and well understood.

Punishments are presumed to reduce the motivation for crime by affecting the cost-benefit calculation of the potential criminal. But most people also have a preventive view of prisons; the phrase, "He ought to be behind bars," often means, "We would all be safer," rather than simply "It would be just what he deserves." The preventive view depends on an analysis of agents—people who would better be shut away—rather than on an analysis of the costs and benefits of crime.

The above analysis is similar to Plato's argument that we could find out what virtue is by examining carefully, in a dialogue, what we already thought. Likewise we urge that people would come up with a pretty complex criminology if posed with cases which require the distinctions we have outlined above. Most people do not automatically think about politics in terms of ideologies; they learn to do so over time with political experience (Converse, 1964, 1970). Likewise, most people do not ordinarily think about simple questions regarding crime with as much theoretical complexity as is possible with cross-examination. When we summarize people's thoughts as "punitive" or "not punitive," this is not a complete description of their cognitive picture of crime.

Problems in Data Interpretation

In Chapter Two we will discuss data on the trends over time in crime, media attention to crime, and public reactions to crime. Briefly, in recent years violent crime has been increasing; media attention to crime has been increasing (until a very recent downturn); the public has become more fearful, more likely to regard crime as a major national problem, and more punitive; and support for gun control has not increased at all.

On the surface, these trends appear consistent with a simple theory that as crime increases, media attention to crime increases; that media attention together with crime increase fear of crime; and that fear of crime evokes increased punitiveness as an attempt to control crime. However, we will see in the examination of the time-series data that even this trend is not at all clear. First, if punitiveness is a solution to crime and increases with increased fear, then gun control, which is obviously directed at crime prevention, should also increase. Second, shifts in the various measures do not correspond in any neat way. It is especially noteworthy that media attention to crime started decreasing long before the crime rate itself started to decline. Finally, some well-known cross-sectional results from the literature on crime suggest opposing hypotheses. For example, low punitiveness is related to other liberal attitudes, so that by and large racial liberals or civil libertarians are less punitive than racial bigots or nonlibertarians. Civil libertarianism has been increasing in recent years (Davis, 1975), as has liberalism in race relations (Taylor, Sheatsley, and Greeley, 1978), in abortion (Evers and McGee, 1977), and in feminism (Smith 1976b); therefore, we would expect a liberal (lenient) trend in the treatment of criminals. In fact we observe the opposite; thus the time-series data contradict the cross-sectional data. That is, the time series suggest that changes that follow one another ought to be causally connected. This concept, which originated with Hume, has its modern expression in attempts to estimate causal models using time-series data (see Land and Felson, 1976). However our time series suggest processes that contradict well-known cross-sectional correlations.

The first problem that emerges from these data concerns the connections among crime, fear of crime, and punitive attitudes. All three series have been increasing in recent years, so it is reasonable that a causal order might be established showing that true crime causes fear of crime, and fear of crime causes people to have punitive reactions, to want to control guns, and in other ways to deal with the crime problem. We immediately face the contradiction that gun control attitudes did not change at all; but there are more difficulties. Women, who are less victimized by violent crime, are more fearful but less punitive than the rest of the white population (a double contradiction). Further, as we will establish in Chapter Three, the cross-sectional relationship between fear of crime and punitiveness is in the right direction, but it is much too small to explain the connection between the two time series.

Chapter Three further explores the indirect causal connection between crime and punitiveness through fear. First we develop an "insurance theory" of the fear of crime, which argues that fear depends on variations in the risks of victimization, on whether those risks are perceived, on the expected loss if one is victimized, and on whether one can take steps to reduce that risk or minimize that loss. This theory connects the increased crime rates to increased fear and helps explain certain obvious discrepancies—such as women being less victimized but more afraid.

The next problem is to see how much increased fear of crime and increased perception of crime as a national problem cause changes in attitudes about punishment. We might imagine that either increased personal fear of victimization or increased perception that other people are being victimized would both produce increased punitiveness. It turns out that both do, but that the differences between fearful and courageous people are not large enough to explain the change over time of punitive attitudes. (Some aspects of this failure of explanation will be addressed in a different way in Chapter Six.)

In each year between 1954 and 1973, 1.6 percent more people gave a liberal response to an average of six civil liberties questions than in the preceding year (Davis, 1975). The trend in race relations items was 1 percent a year in the liberal direction, with a spurt in the early 1970s to 3 percent per year (Taylor, Sheatsley, and Greeley, 1978). This massive shift in public opinion on core liberal issues is probably the biggest value change recorded in the short history of survey research. As we will demonstrate in Chapter Four, lenience toward criminals is part of the liberal world view; therefore such a massive shift in public views might have been expected to carry along with it a general loosening in the attitude toward punishment of criminals. But, as we have observed, punitiveness toward criminals has increased during the latest part of this period. Thus, we have two parts of the liberal world view moving in opposite directions.

This disparity suggests that we do not really understand the correlation between lenience toward criminals and the liberal world view that produces the cross-sectional data. It also suggests that the process of change in opinion on punitiveness might be different for people with a generally liberal world view than it is for conservatives. This latter suggestion is reinforced by certain anomalies in the cross-sectional data, such as the fact that the most conservative region-by-sex group on race relations, Southern women, are the most lenient on the question of capital punishment.

Chapter Four takes up this problem of different parts of the liberal world view moving in different directions by trying to specify the connection between general liberalism and punitiveness. The interaction of region, race, and sex with time on the relationship between attitudes towards race relations and punitiveness and between busing and punitiveness are also examined.

Chapter Five takes up the contradiction that gun control

attitudes have not changed during a period in which other attitudes that reflect "solutions to the crime problem" have increased. In order to understand gun control attitudes, we find that we have to understand gun ownership. The strongest determinant of whether one favors gun control is whether one is a gun owner. The strongest determinant of being a gun owner is being a hunter; and being a hunter is associated with being male, with rural life, and with living in regions where hunting is popular. Gun-owning regions, and gun owners, have certain cultural characteristics; for example, they are likely to be Protestant and to favor capital punishment. The conclusion is that our explanatory problem concerns not the crime problem but the defense of a rural hunting culture. That culture has views about what should be done with criminals (they should be severely punished) and is also situated where the victimization rates are much lower (rural areas) and where people are therefore not afraid of crime. The result is that much of the punitive reaction to crime that one would expect to be concentrated in cities (where there is more crime and fear of crime) is instead concentrated in the countryside. Another result is that opposition to gun control is concentrated in exactly those places in which the recent rise in violent crime has had the least impact. The most fearful group (and the group whose fear has increased the most), women living in large cities, was already nearly 100 percent in favor of gun registration; there is no room for further change. Men in rural areas, who are most likely to own guns, were not very afraid earlier and did not become much more afraid. They formed the backbone of opposition to gun control, and it is their nonmovement that explains the consistent 25 percent of the public against gun registration.

The overall result of Chapters Three, Four, and Five is to leave us even more puzzled about the contradictions raised by the time series. It is clear that none of these dynamics at the individual level are sufficient to explain the movement of punitive attitudes. The increase in fear is not large enough to explain the movement of punitiveness over time; the increase in liberalism should push punitiveness in the opposite direction from that in which it has gone; and the data on gun control and

gun ownership show that a rural hunting culture, which has
among its features a slight tendency to punitiveness, shows no
sign of increase or decline. By elimination, then, it seems that
we have to move to collective forces—to movements of public
opinion as a whole and to their causes—to explain these recent
developments. The problem this poses is how one can get
measurements at a collective level in cross-sectional data. We
have only one society moving through recent American experience, and while one case is a very much larger sample than
none, the time-series data themselves do not speak very clearly
and uniformly about what collective process might be going on.

Chapter Six exploits one opportunity for collective level
measurements: the fact that our respondents come from neighborhoods with characteristics that predict very different rates
of crime and victimization. As we will demonstrate in Chapter
Three, people who live in larger cities and people who live
near black people (especially including other black people)
show higher levels of victimization and higher levels of fear
of crime. That is, urban integrated and ghetto neighborhoods
show every evidence of being areas in which the salience
of crime is very high, and they therefore differ from small
town segregated neighborhoods in the same way that the United
States as a whole differs in recent years from the United States
a decade or more ago.

Two problems are of interest: We have shown above that
as the United States became more afraid of crime, it became
more punitive. We can therefore study whether when neighborhoods as collectives become more punitive they also become more afraid of crime. Second, we have shown, and will
explore in more detail in Chapter Four, that as collective fear
increases, two aspects of the liberal world view move in opposite directions. One hypothesis therefore is that as crime
becomes more salient, something happens to the relation between general world views and opinions on lenience and punitiveness. A hypothesis suggested by cognitive consistency
theory would hold, for example, that as the salience of a subject
like crime increases, one's response to that problem would be
more likely to agree with one's general world view. For example,

it might be that in the face of increased crime and fear, lenience toward criminals could only be maintained by hard-core liberals, so that the correlation between lenience and liberalism might increase. Thus, in neighborhoods in which there is high fear of crime (inner-city neighborhoods in large cities), we might expect higher correlations among punitive attitudes and higher correlations between liberalism on other questions and lenience toward criminals. Likewise it may also be that education specifies the correlation between punitiveness and civil liberties. Chapter Six then, is directed at the analysis of this one source of collective variation which can be studied with cross-sectional data, and so can illuminate the collective movement of public opinion, which could not be explained by individual-level analyses.

The analysis in this book borrows ideas from many theoretical perspectives in behavioral research. In Chapter Seven we summarize the main findings in the book and then relate them to the general theoretical questions from the fields of public choice, social psychology, survey methodology, public opinion, and policy research that guided our inquiry.

2

Trends in Crime Rates, Media Coverage, and Public Opinion

Crime is a pervasive social problem that reaches into and alters the lives of large numbers of people in the United States. Even when people have not themselves had direct experience with crime, it frequently affects indirectly the ways in which they travel, the extent to which they go out at night, and the ways in which they perceive their neighborhoods. People cope with the crime problem in various ways: they become afraid, stay indoors, move to the suburbs, buy locks and guard dogs, and do not interact with strangers. Many of these private solutions have major consequences for the quality of life generally, but they are not considered matters of public policy. Public solutions to the crime problem take other forms: crime detection, law enforcement, punishment, and research on crime. This book examines public opinion about public solutions; our goal is to explain the relationship between private experience and public opinion on public remedies.

To begin we will consider the way in which public opinion on the question of crime and punishment has changed in recent years. In this chapter we report a number of trends related in one way or another to the problem of crime and punishment and to public response to that problem. We will find that aside from the reportorial purpose of these data, they pose a series of explanatory problems. The trends we will analyze in this chapter show the following:

1. Crime—particularly violent crime—has been increasing.
2. At the same time, fear of crime has been increasing, and that increase is greater among women than among men.
3. The perception of crime as a major national problem has also been increasing in the same period.
4. A series of social attitudes (including those on race relations and civil liberties), which are negatively correlated with punitive attitudes, have been moving in a liberal direction over the same period. Thus, if general liberalism produces lenience toward criminals, punitiveness should have been going down, not up.
5. Finally, support for gun control has not been going down or up but has remained constant.

In isolation, some of these recent trends suggest the following causal theory: Violent crime makes people afraid, so an increase in crime causes an increase in fear; and increased fear and increased perception of crime as a public problem increase punitiveness. However, some trends directly contradict these explanations. For example, if people want to control violent crime by more punitiveness, why do they not want to control it by more gun control? Other trends exhibit conflicting evidence on causal connections: If more liberal people are more lenient, why does the increase in the number of liberals and intensity of liberal sentiment not lead to more lenience (less punitiveness) toward criminals? As a set, then, the time trends do not give rise to a clear causal picture.

To further complicate the issue, we find that the relationships among these variables at the individual level (for example, the degree to which a fearful person is more punitive)

are not large enough to explain the aggregate change in punitiveness, even when they are in the right direction. This suggests that there may be causal relations at the collective level—
that societies more concerned with crime will develop a more
punitive public opinion as a collectivity.

It is unfortunate that survey questions tapping public
reaction to crime and punishment have appeared mainly since
crime has become a salient public problem. The FBI Uniform
Crime Reports and the *Reader's Guide to Periodical Literature*
tell us about crime rates and the volume of media coverage of
crime, but we do not have comparable periodic measurements
of attitudes on crime. Therefore we have examined surveys
that have asked about fear of crime, the most important problem faced by the country, capital punishment, severity of
courts, and gun control. These questions have imperfect time
series, but the available data can be pieced together to reveal
certain trends.

Changes in the Crime Rate Over Time

In order to determine what causes public attention to
crime to fluctuate over time, we must find what sorts of crime
make people afraid. This assumes that salience is a function of
fear, and that the increase in fear-producing crime is the element of the overall crime increase that evokes public attention.
Although about 15 percent of all arrests in 1975 were for the
"crime" of drunkenness, people presumably do not get excited
enough about this to favor capital punishment. Fear-producing crime is violent crime (this will be examined further in
Chapter Three).

Closely connected to the question of what makes people
afraid is the problem of accuracy in crime measurement over
time. In measuring the increase in crime, we would rather omit
crimes for which the definition or degree of moral culpability
has changed. We would also like to omit crimes whose recording
is affected by variables such as the urbanization of the population or the bureaucratization of law enforcement. (Large,
urban police departments have more complete records for

certain less serious crime categories.) From the point of view of measurement comparability, the murder rate is the most reliable measure. However, the broad pattern of change in the murder rate compared with the change in the overall violent crime rate indicates that the murder rate is not a good measure of fear-producing crime. (The data from the FBI Uniform Crime Reports are available in the U.S. Bureau of the Census, *Statistical Abstract,* 1976, and in U.S. Bureau of the Census, *Historical Statistics,* 1975). The relationship between the murder rate and the overall rate of violent crime has changed substantially over time; the murder rate was about one twentieth of the recorded crime rate in 1933 and about one fortieth in the 1970s. (The arrest rate for murder is twice as high because most murderers are arrested but only about half of all other violent criminals are arrested.) Unless we are willing to admit that the reporting rate for rapes, aggravated assaults, and robberies doubled between the 1930s and 1970s, the composition of crimes of violence has been changing. If we use the murder rate alone in diagnosing the crime problem, then the situation was about the same in the 1970s as it was in the early 1930s. If we use the rate of violent crime as a whole, then the 1970s have about twice as serious a crime problem as the 1930s. The violent crime that has increased most in relation to murder is robbery: the ratio of robberies to murders nearly tripled between 1957 and 1970 (calculated from U.S. Bureau of the Census, 1975, series H-954 and H-956). As we will see later, it is especially among people disproportionately exposed to robbery (those in large cities living in integrated or all-black neighborhoods) who are most afraid of walking near their homes. Thus, the increase in the basis for fear is measured better by the total number of violent crimes than by the total number of murders. In fact, this total-crime criterion indicates that the most recent peak of concern with crime was grounded in an actual increase in crime.

The rates of violent crime per 100,000 population known to the police from 1933 to 1975 are presented in Table 1. The trend begins with a decline in the early 1930s that continues during the war years. This decline is followed by a sharp increase immediately after the war, which leads to a

Table 1. Total Reported Murders, Rapes, Robberies, and
Aggravated Assaults per 100,000 Population, 1933-1975

Year	Violent crime rate	Year	Violent crime rate
1933	177	1955	136
1934	151	1956	137
		1957	141
1935	134	1958	148
1936	122	1959	147
1937	124		
1938	120	1960	160
1939	118	1961	157
		1962	161
1940	115	1963	167
1941	112	1964	189
1942	113		
1943	109	1965	198
1944	114	1966	218
		1967	251
1945	132	1968	295
1946	142	1969	325
1947	140		
1948	136	1970	361
1949	138	1971	393
		1972	398
1950	133	1973	417
1951	128	1974	461
1952	139		
1953	146	1975	482
1954	147		

Source: Office of Management and Budget, 1973, Table 211; supplemental
data from U.S. Bureau of the Census, 1976, Table 252. Figures are rounded to the
nearest digit.

new plateau with fluctuations. One of the fluctuations reaches
a peak around 1955. An accelerating increase starts around
1960 and continues until 1976, where there is a hint of a
downturn (U.S. Bureau of the Census, 1975 [series H-971],
1976). The murder rate also varies: Following a peak of 9.7
per 100,000 in 1933, the murder rate declined to only 5 per
100,000 in 1944, jumping to 6.4 in 1946. After decreasing to
below 5 per 100,000 again for all years but one between 1951

and 1963, the murder rate climbed again in the 1960s, passing
7.0 in 1968 and reaching 8.7 in 1975. Because the ratio of
murders to total violent crime has shrunk, the recent exponen-
tial increase in violent crime must consist in large measure of
increases in robbery and aggravated assault. (On the reliability
of the crime reports from police records, see Smith, 1977.)

It is important to keep Table 1 in proper perspective.
A very small fraction of the population commits serious crimes,
even in the most recent years in our time series. Only about 4.5
percent of the population in 1975 were arrested for some
offense other than a traffic violation. (This is a rate of arrests
per year, so the proportion is actually slightly lower.) Of these,
less than a quarter, or 1.1 percent of the population, were
arrested for "serious offenses," ranging from murder to motor
vehicle theft. Of those arrested for "serious offenses," roughly
one fifth were accused of violent crimes such as murder, rape,
robbery, and aggravated assault. Therefore, about 0.2 percent
of the population were arrested for serious crimes of violence.
Of these serious violent crimes, about one twentieth involved
murder or nonnegligent manslaughter, creating a population rate
of about .01 percent, or one in 10,000. In other words, very
few people have been arrested for serious offenses, in spite of
the dramatic increases in crime.

Likewise, the great surge in crime does not mean that
Americans are continually being attacked. Victimization studies,
which measure incidence of crime independent of police accounts, suggest that only about 1.8 percent of the population
over twelve years old in 1973-1974 experienced any violent
crime in a given year (U.S. Bureau of the Census, 1976, Table
257). That is, the average person could expect to go for fifty
years and be raped, robbed, or battered only once. On one
hand, of course, once is too often; further, these data do not
take into account the fact that victimization is very unequally
distributed—a young black male living in a large city may be
lucky to get through one year without being victimized. On the
other hand, the victimization rate of once every fifty years
only characterizes the peak in recent years: All but ten of the
past forty years have had a crime rate less than half that during

the period when the victimization studies were done. Therefore, if we assume that the relationship between actual victimization and reported crime is the same for all the years in our study, then people in the 1930s, 1940s, 1950s, and early 1960s were victimized less than once in every 100 years of life. A great surge of certain violent crimes (especially robbery) in the late 1960s and early 1970s brought this victimization rate to about once in fifty years. Although the increase has been proportionally very large, this still affects a relatively small part of the population in a given year.

Changes in Media Coverage over Time

The topical index of the *Reader's Guide to Periodical Literature* has had a category called "Crime and Criminals" since the arbitrary beginning of our analysis in 1933. While normal changes in both editorial policy and titling articles will cause variations in the meaning of this category over time, the number of articles per month provides a rough measure of the salience of crime in magazines. It is not clear how far this reflects salience in the media generally, but one's casual impression is that the media are similar in the attention they give to various topics. Thus Table 2 indicates major shifts in the amount of media attention to crime and criminals, although the data used are very rough.

The attention paid to crime in the periodical literature has not remained constant over time. There have been four "bulges" in the amount of periodical literature devoted to crime between 1933 and 1974. The low points have shown one to two articles per month; the high points reach just over four articles per month. If we consider a "bulge" to be 2.5 or more articles per month as indexed by the *Reader's Guide* "Crime and Criminals" section, then we find a Depression peak starting in 1933 and lasting until 1936, a postwar peak from 1949 to 1955, a 1960s peak from 1965 to 1969, and a 1970s peak from 1974 to 1976. The wave-like progression suggests that journalists or the public get tired of articles on the same subject but that a few years' respite recharges their interest.

These four peaks of media attention correspond roughly

Table 2. Trends in Periodical Literature on
"Crime and Criminals"

Beginning Date of Reader's Guide to Periodical Literature Volume	Average number of articles per month[a]
June, 1932	4.3
June, 1935	2.8
June, 1937	1.8
June, 1939	1.7
June, 1941	1.1
June, 1943	1.0
April, 1945	2.2
April, 1947	2.4
April, 1949	3.7
March, 1951	4.1
March, 1953	3.0
February, 1955	2.3
February, 1957	1.9
February, 1959	2.5
February, 1961	1.4
February, 1963	2.0
February, 1965	3.9
February, 1966	3.7
February, 1967	4.6
February, 1968	3.3
February, 1969	2.6
February, 1970	1.9
February, 1971	2.2
February, 1972	2.0
February, 1973	1.8
February, 1974	3.0
February, 1975	3.3

Source: *Reader's Guide to Periodical Literature,* various issues.

[a]The count of articles under "Crime and Criminals" was divided by the number of months covered by the volume.

to peaks in the murder rate and to periods of increased violent crime. However, the length and timing of media peaks do not correlate closely with these crime rate fluctuations; further, the decline in the number of articles devoted to crime between 1970 and 1974, during a period of increasing violent crimes, is a contradictory trend. The linear correlation between the amount of crime and media attention for each year is not very great, and formal statistical analysis would show that there is very little to be learned about one trend from the other.

Changes in the Salience of Crime

Periodically since 1946, the Gallup polls have asked people to describe in their own words the "most important problem" in the country (see Smith, 1976a). The Gallup organization codes these with a set of categories that change as the focus of public attention shifts. While this violates rigorous standards of measurement, there is no systematic way to measure the shifting focus of public attention. The reason is that the focus of public attention shifts substantively over time, thus changing the meaning of certain categories. For example, it is not clear when the Vietnam War was best coded as a subvariety of the "foreign policy" category and when it became a separate category in its own right. Because we do not know any better way to measure "most important problem," we will use the percentages of people mentioning problems in the Gallup categories to indicate the salience of crime (compared with other matters) in public opinion. The exact wording and data sources for the Gallup question (and for all other survey questions analyzed in this book) are shown in the Appendix.

The percentage of the public indicating that "crime" or "juvenile delinquency" was the "most important problem" is shown in Table 3. Note that these are small percentages taken from samples with about 1,400 respondents. By random sampling standards, the standard error of 2 percent should be about .4 percent; however, since these are clustered samples we might expect the standard error to be about .6 percent. The standard error of the difference might therefore be about .8 percent. Fluctuations, then, have to be above 1.6 percent to be taken very seriously. Thus the surge of interest in 1960 and 1962 was probably not a sampling fluctuation, and the great surge of salience of crime after 1969 indicates a reliable shift in public attention to crime and delinquency.

The impression one gets from comparing this trend to the preceding two is that the great surge of public interest (salience) corresponds to the great surge in crime much better than to the periodic surges of media attention to crime and criminals. People seem to respond more sensibly than the media to the

Table 3. Trends in Naming Crime as the Most Important Problem

Year	Percent
1946	0
1947	0
1948	0
1949	0
1950	0.5
1951	0
1954	0.9
1955	0
1956	.010
1957	.016
1958	.004
1959	.005
1960	.028
1962	.028
1963	0
1964	0
1965	.026
1966	.015
1967	.013
1968	.037
1969	.061
1970	.067
1971	.072
1972	.069
1973	.068

Source: Gallup Polls. When more than one study was available in a single year, the data from those studies were averaged.

scope of the crime problem. (See, however, contrary evidence in Davis, 1952.)

The question, "Is there any area right around here—that is, within a mile—where you would be afraid to walk alone at night?" has been asked by the Gallup polls six times since the middle 1960s and has also been included in the 1973, 1974, 1976, and 1977 General Social Surveys. However, because data are available for only this short time period, they reflect nothing about long-run trends of public and media attention to crime. For the period since 1965, the series shows a significant linear trend, with an increase of fear of .42 percentage points annually. Most of this change occurred between 1967 and 1974. (See Taylor, 1980, for a description of the weighted regression technique used for analyzing trends in public opinion.)

Table 4 shows the trend over time separately for the two sexes. The trend for females shows some fluctuations in the 1960s around the level of 50 percent afraid, then increases and fluctuates around 60 percent during the 1970s. There is a slight upward trend for males. The overall picture is simplified if we consolidate the three Gallup polls from the 1960s and the four General Social Surveys for the 1970s. It is clear that fear of crime has increased for both sexes, 4.6 percent for men and 12.3 percent for women. The increase for women is significantly larger than that for men, indicating that the increase in violent crime damages the quality of life of women more than of men.

Table 4. Trends in Fear, by Sex

		Percentage afraid	
Survey	Date	Male	Female
Gallup	3/65	18.4 (711)[a]	52.2 (763)
Gallup	8/67	16.4 (793)	45.9 (795)
Gallup	9/68	19.3 (729)	50.7 (738)
GSS	3/73	20.0 (696)	59.6 (792)
GSS	3/74	24.1 (688)	63.4 (784)
GSS	3/76	23.1 (666)	60.9 (826)
GSS	3/77	23.4 (688)	63.1 (832)

[a]Raw frequencies indicated in parentheses.

The concentration of violent crime in the ghetto is reflected in the racial difference in fear of the streets. The data from the four General Social Surveys are consolidated in Table 5. We see that blacks of both sexes are more afraid than whites. Among males, blacks are 16.4 percent more afraid than whites; among females, blacks are 12.4 percent more afraid than whites. These racial differences within genders are not significant.

Table 5. Percentage Afraid in Four Surveys from the 1970s
by Race and Sex

| Sex | Race | | |
	Black	White	Other
Male	37.4 (286)[a]	21.0 (2,431)	14.3 (21)
Female	72.8 (368)	60.4 (2,845)	57.1 (21)

Source: General Social Surveys, 1973-1974 and 1976-1977 combined.

[a]Raw frequencies indicated in parentheses.

Trends in the Solution to Crime

In the following three sections, we will analyze changing trends in solutions to the crime problem from three perspectives: changes in public attitudes toward punitiveness, changes in actual punitive measures taken toward criminals, and gun control.

Punitive Attitudes over Time. Two survey questions that have been repeated over time give us some idea about how people think criminals should be treated. The first concerns capital punishment for murder, and the second asks whether the local courts should be harsher in punishing criminals. (Exact wordings appear in the Appendix.) Table 6 shows the percentages of people *approving* capital punishment for persons convicted of murder, with the "don't know's" *excluded.* (The Gallup polls record more "don't know's" than the General Social Surveys.) We see high support for capital punishment in the 1930s and high support on a repeat measurement in 1953. Thereafter there is more fluctuation and more frequent measurement; in general,

Table 6. Trends in Capital Punishment Attitudes

Survey	Date	Percent in favor
Gallup	4/36	62.0
	11/36	61.0
	11/37	60.0
	11/53[a]	63.8
	4/56	53.4
	9/57	47.4
	3/60	52.7
	2/65	45.4
	7/66	42.0
	6/67	55.7
	1/69	51.3
	10/71	48.2
	2/72	50.9
GSS	3/72	53.0
	3/73	60.2
	3/74	63.0
	3/75	60.1
	3/76	65.5
	4/76	66.6
	3/77	67.2

Source: Smith, 1976b, p. 261.

[a]The categories "qualified yes" and "qualified no" were grouped with the "don't know's."

attitudes became less punitive. In the middle 1960s, the surges in public concern with crime, in media attention, and in personal fear reversed this trend, pushing capital punishment in a punitive direction. The great crime wave of the late 1960s and early 1970s made people nearly as punitive toward murderers as they were in the 1950s and as punitive as they were in the 1930s.

This is, of course, only one way of reading the trend. From a technical point of view, the earlier data are too far apart to serve as time series at all. We find fluctuations over short periods of time (for example, from 1972 to 1974) that are as large as the difference between the level in the 1930s and that in the 1960s. Thus we have no way of knowing whether our measure in 1953, for example, was at the end or the beginning of a fluctuation like that between 1972 or 1974 or whether instead it represents the general level of punitiveness of the early 1950s. When major fluctuations occur at unevenly spaced intervals, a series of data points does not adequately characterize the historical movement.

The part of the time series that we can interpret most assuredly, then, is only the most recent section. Punitiveness was relatively low in 1965 but underwent an unsteady increase until 1977. A sharp rise in punitiveness occurred between 1966 and 1967 followed by a move away from punitiveness until 1972. Punitiveness then increased between 1972 and 1977. While the overall recent trend in punitiveness is definitely upward, the veering of public opinion during a time of great public concern over crime and criminals indicates that the salience of crime does not automatically lead to punitiveness. This lack of correlation is supported by the fact that the percentage of people mentioning crime as a major national problem in the 1950s was very low, while the level of punitiveness was very high.

Smith (1976c) analyzed the trends in capital punishment attitudes for many subgroups of the population. These subgroups changed at the same rate, with three exceptions: sex, race, and political party preference. Although women and men have been, on the average, 11.5 percentage points apart on this question, that difference shrank to 7.5 percent in 1974. (This apparent convergence may have been a sampling fluctuation, however.) In contrast, blacks and whites have been moving further away from each other on this issue at a rate of 1.1 percent per year since 1953. Through the entire time series, blacks have been less likely to favor capital punishment and have shown little change. A linear trend of this difference shows the gap between the races to have been 6.4 percent in 1953 and 29.9 percent in 1974. In the final exception, political Independents have changed their position relative to the Republicans and Democrats. In 1953, Independents were more similar to Republicans (who, on the average, have been about 9.8 percent more likely to favor capital punishment than Democrats). In the 1970s, however, Independents were more similar to Democrats in their propensity to oppose capital punishment.

Aside from these exceptions, the other correlates of capital punishment do not "interact" with time; that is, the relationship between sociodemographic variables and attitudes toward capital punishment remain constant over the course of our time series. Throughout the period, high-income people are 13.4 percent more likely to favor capital punishment than low-income people, after one has controlled for education. Having more education is correlated with opposing capital punishment; attending college makes an estimated difference of 7.3 percent over never graduating from high school. Well-to-do people with less than a high school education are consequently predicted to be 20.7 percent more punitive than college-educated people with low incomes. In addition, the youngest cohort in our analysis, born between 1940 and 1955, was more lenient by 10.0 percent than other cohorts. These relationships are fairly steady over time.

Before interpreting these patterns, we will supplement them with responses to the survey question: "In general, do you think the courts in this area deal too harshly or not harshly enough with criminals?" The response categories were "too harshly," "not harshly enough," and "about right" (though the third answer was not specified in the question itself). Combining the replications from the 1972, 1973, and 1974 General Social Surveys, we can estimate an overall relationship between this question and the capital punishment question. Those who answered "not harshly enough" (the punitive answer) were 24.3 percent more likely to support capital punishment for murder than those who said "about right." Those who said "about right," in turn, were 10.1 percent more likely to support capital punishment than those who said their local courts were "too harsh" (data for three years combined). There is, then, a very strong correlation between these two items, indicating that capital punishment and tough courts are manifestations of a general tendency to be punitive toward criminals. Therefore, the courts question, for the briefer time span it covers, can supplement our knowledge of the time trend of punitiveness derived from the capital punishment question.

Table 7 shows the percentage of people answering "not harsh enough" over time. The surge of punitiveness on this issue appears between 1965 and 1967 with another increase after 1973. This means that the increase in punitiveness on this item seem to coincide better with the surge of media attention to crime and criminals between 1965 and 1968 than with the increase in public concern.

Table 7. Trends in Attitudes Toward the Courts

Survey	Date	Percentage saying courts are "not harsh enough"
Gallup	3/65	48.9
Gallup	9/65	59.3
Gallup	1/68	63.1
Gallup	1/69	74.4
GSS	3/72	74.4
Gallup	12/72	66.3
GSS	3/73	73.1
GSS	3/74	77.9
GSS	3/75	79.2
GSS	3/76	81.0
GSS	3/77	83.0
GSS	3/78	84.9

Between 1965 and 1974, the sex difference in response to this question has been narrowing at the rate of about 1.0 percent per year. In 1965, 53.6 percent of the women surveyed endorsed harsher courts and 61.5 percent of men did, resulting in a sex difference of 7.9 percent. By 1974, 84.8 percent of the women were punitive compared with 88.1 percent of the men—only a 3.3 percent difference.

Similarly, the educational differences decreased during this period, with college respondents approaching high school respondents at the rate of 1.45 percent per year. The general pattern, then, was one of shrinking differences among the population in the degree of punitiveness expressed. Much of the change represented in Table 7 consists of a move toward punitiveness by groups that were lenient in 1965.

Punitiveness changes at a different rate for blacks than for whites. Taking into account the results of the capital punishment question, it appears that blacks were not becoming more punitive at the same rate as whites during this period.

The overall impression from these two rather spotty time series—attitudes on capital punishment and the courts—is that increased salience of crime is associated with increased punitiveness in the most recent years. Increased salience has homogenized the white population behind a law-and-order position, although our evidence also shows that salience of crime and punitiveness have not necessarily moved together at all points in time. Blacks, in contrast, have evidently become increasingly suspicious of whether "law and order" is good for them, perhaps suspecting that it is merely a subtle way for white people to be prejudiced against black people. It is true that the recent large increases in violent crimes known to the police have resulted in disproportionately more black arrests, so an increase in punitiveness will in fact fall disproportionately on the black community.

Objective Punitiveness. Though the survey questions have been the same over time, the actual punitiveness of the justice system has been changing. In this section we will describe the changes in objective punitiveness and discuss the implications of these changes for changes in social control attitudes.

If we estimate the punitiveness of the American justice system from official statistical sources, we find that it has been decreasing. We can estimate the years of prison served per 1,000 civilian population by using the percentage of the population in state or federal prisons at the beginning of the year. This gives a figure of .976 years in prison per 1,000 population years in 1970 and 1.036 years in prison per 1,000 population years in 1975. These figures are quite similar and show that on the average about one in every 1,000 civilians is in prison in the United States at any given time.

The rate of incarceration was roughly constant during this period, although the rate of serious crime was increasing. Calculating the arrest rate for reporting districts in 1970, we obtain 8.403 arrests for serious crimes per 1,000 population;

for 1975 the corresponding figure is 11.580 arrests per 1,000 population. Though there is a larger increase here than in the incarceration rate, we see that, during this period, the arrest rate is fairly stable. Roughly one in every 100 people is arrested each year for a serious crime.

If we divide the rate of incarceration by the arrest rate, we get the average punishment per serious crime arrest. This average punishment per arrest is one tenth of a year in prison. But because there is a stronger increase in the arrest figures than in the incarceration figures, the sentence served per serious crime arrest has decreased: The average serious crime arrest resulted in about .116 years of sentence served in state or federal prisons in 1970; in 1975 this had dropped to .089 years of incarceration per arrest (U.S. Bureau of the Census, 1972, Tables 236 and 264; 1976, Tables 272 and 291; estimates are not statistically satisfactory because of changing coverage of crime statistics). In short, during a period in which people were becoming more concerned about crime, more afraid to walk near their homes at night, and more supportive of punitive policies (as we demonstrated earlier in this chapter), the government was actually implementing a more lenient policy. While the voters were demanding harsher penalties for crime and while politicians were responding to that shift in public opinion with law-and-order speeches, the average prison sentence per arrest was dropping, and capital punishment of murderers remained at the same level (that is, there were no executions).

These data are important in relation to the survey question about the courts, which reads, "In general, do you think the courts in this area deal too harshly or not harshly enough with criminals?" We have just shown that the courts, in conjunction with the rest of the corrections system, were becoming less harsh in their dealings with criminals. The objective meaning of the question was therefore changing over time: Respondents were being asked to compare their ideal levels of harshness with a shifting real level of harshness of the justice system. It is not clear whether people pay enough attention to the details of court and corrections policies to be able to detect a 25 percent decrease in the average prison sentence per arrest. Given the

ambiguity of the question, therefore, we cannot really be sure
whether the increasing punitiveness of respondents represents
a desire for a substantial increase in penalties for crime or a desire for the courts to return to their earlier level of punitiveness.

   Gun Control. Table 8 illustrates media attention to gun
control laws and attempts at gun regulation as measured by
Reader's Guide citations. There was little attention to this
issue through 1963, although there has been sustained attention
at the rate of about one article per month since then. A large
spurt in media attention occurred in 1967 to 1968, concurrent
with the passage of Gun Control Act of 1968. This peak also
coincides approximately with the peak of media attention to
crime and criminals, though there is no evidence of comparable
peaks in the early 1930s or after World War II similar to those
we found for attention to crime and criminals.

   Gun control has only recently become statistically related
to the problem of increases in violent crime. For example, the
higher murder rate of 1933 did not produce media concern with
gun registration. But has the media's connection of the crime
problem with gun control resulted in a comparable movement
of public opinion favoring the registration of guns? Table 9
shows the percentages of people endorsing two types of gun
control legislation. The first asks whether people favor a gun
control measure that requires a police permit for owning a
gun. The second asks whether guns should be registered at the
time of sale. If people become more inclined to endorse gun
control as the crime problem becomes more severe (as they
have become more likely to endorse harsh sentences and capital
punishment), this percentage endorsing gun control should
increase between 1965 and 1970, as punitiveness does. But
there is no evidence of such an increase: On both gun control
series, the portion of the population approving runs very close
to 75 percent at all time points.

   The parts of the population who support gun control are
different enough in their other attitudes on punitiveness to indicate that if gun control is a solution to the crime problem,
its social supports are completely different from the social
supports of punitiveness. For instance, women—for whom the

Table 8. Trends in Periodical Literature on Gun Control

Beginning date	Average number of articles per month
June 1932	.11
June 1935	0
June 1937	.04
June 1939	.12
June 1941	0
June 1943	0
April 1945	0
April 1947	0
April 1949	0
March 1951	0
March 1953	0
February 1955	.08
February 1957	.21
February 1959	.12
February 1961	.04
February 1963	.875
February 1965	1.08
February 1966	1.17
February 1967	1.67
February 1968	.92
February 1969	.58
February 1970	.58
February 1971	.83
February 1972	1.17
February 1973	.75
February 1974	.83
February 1975	

Source: Reader's Guide to Periodical Literature, various issues. The count of articles under "Firearms–Laws and Regulations" was divided by the number of months covered by the volume.

crime problem is more salient than it is for men—endorse solving the crime problem with gun control 17.1 percent more than men (on the average over ten studies), while they endorse harsher courts somewhat less and capital punishment a lot less than men. The hypothesis that gun control is a completely different sort of social control question is further supported by the very large effects of community size. Different sized communities (as we will see in Chapter Six) do not differ appreciably in punitiveness. But large metropolitan areas are from 21.6 percent (in the exurbs) to 22.8 percent (in large central

Table 9. Trends in Attitudes Toward Gun Control

		Percentage favoring gun control by:	
Survey	Year	Police permit	Registration of sales
Gallup	1959	77.9	
Gallup	1963	81.8	
Gallup, Gallup	1965	75.4, 73.9	
Gallup	1966	69.5	
Gallup	1967	74.8	
Gallup	1968		76.0
Gallup	1971	74.7	
GSS, Gallup	1972	72.4, 74.0	
GSS	1973	74.8	
GSS	1974	76.2	
GSS, Gallup	1975	75.6	75.0
GSS	1976	72.6	
GSS	1977	73.0	

cities) more favorably inclined toward gun control than are people who live in the open country or in small towns (General Social Surveys, 1974 and 1975 combined). Other differences on this question can be explained by this community type difference in endorsement of gun control; for example, Jews and Catholics are much more in favor of gun control than Protestants because Jews and Catholics are more likely to live in cities. Because the gun control time trend is not coherently related to the increased salience of crime or increased punitiveness, it will be dealt with separately in Chapter Five.

Summary

The preceding time series trace the variations over time in actual crime, in the salience of crime in the public mind, and in possible solutions to the crime problem. The broad pattern— with a good many caveats and exceptions—is that periods with high or increasing violent crime rates tend to be associated with a surge of attention to crime and criminals in the media. Either the crime rate itself or the media attention it receives seems to increase public sentiment that there is a national crime problem, though the weight of the evidence is that people pay more attention to the true crime rate than to the level of media coverage. As far as one can tell from recent developments in fear of crime, the radical increase in the crime rate observed by the police (and reported in the FBI Uniform Crime Reports) is also observed by the people, and it frightens them. That is, crime becomes more salient in one's personal life as the crime rate increases.

The recent increase in the salience of crime has apparently been associated with an increase in punitiveness toward criminals. The significant exception to this is that black people, it appears, have not become more punitive. And—again with the exception of blacks—the population is apparently becoming more homogeneous as well as more punitive in its attitudes toward criminals, because it is less differentiated by sex and education now than previously.

Some peculiarities arise from these time series curves, although most of them are not sufficiently long or do not have sufficiently frequent measurements to be judged accurately. It is very difficult to see any regular time pattern or over-time association between crime and salience for the media, between salience in the media and salience in the public mind, and between salience in the public mind and punitiveness. In addition, in spite of the massive changes in the position of crime in the public mind as well as in media attention to gun control, public support of gun registration or police permits has been stable at about 75 percent.

The series of trends can be considered "social indicators" in the field of crime and the public reaction to crime. Comparatively speaking, they are fairly good social indicators for opinion items. The capital punishment series is one of the longest series in existence for a public opinion question. With all their shortcomings, the Uniform Crime Reports are among the best measures available on the size of a given social problem. Both the *Reader's Guide* and the "most important problem" series are also fairly long, as public opinion series go.

The methodological difficulty we face is that our conclusions about causality are drawn from fluctuations in time series, and there are too few fluctuations. If these series contained enough fluctuations to be informative, then one could study the relationship between the fluctuations in different series with any degree of formality that one pleased. Given the sparsity of relevant information for over-time causal analysis, we will turn to cross-sectional analysis to develop and test theories of how these variables are related to each other.

3

Fear of Crime and Views on Punishment

. . . .
. . . .
. . . .

Much of social science is concerned with explaining the obvious —either showing that the obvious is actually not true, that it is only part of the truth, or that it is only true because of subtle and complex processes operating below the surface. In this chapter we try to explain two obvious things: that crime makes people afraid and that fear makes people more punitive. As it turns out, both of these statements are true, but neither is adequate in itself. Crime does make people afraid, but it makes some people more afraid than others. For example, though women are the victims of crime less often than men, they are more afraid. And, though fear does make people advocate harsher punishment of criminals, fearful people are in general only slightly more punitive than others, and some fearful groups—like women and blacks—are less punitive. What we have to explain, then, is why the obvious is only partly true.

Why Crime Causes Fear

Fear can be defined as the perception by a person of high risk of serious damage, which the person can do nothing to alleviate or control. Violent street crime produces fear, but other crimes and accidents that may result in comparable objective losses do not elicit nearly as much fear. In this chapter we attempt to show why this is the case through a series of strategic comparisons between violent street crime and other sources of risk. These comparisons serve two related functions: They illustrate our definition of fear and they relate this general definition to fear of crime.

When we speak of *risk*, we are referring to the probability that an individual will experience a given level of loss or damage; we are thus holding constant the seriousness of the damage involved. In discussing risk and the perception of risk—two components of our definition of fear—we will compare the risk of death by automobile accident to the risk of death during a robbery on the street.

Objectively the risk of being killed in an automobile accident in a given year runs between two and four times the risk of any kind of murder. One is more likely to be murdered by someone one knows than to be murdered by a stranger during a robbery. This means that one's objective risk of being killed in a motor vehicle accident is four to ten times as great as one's risk of being murdered by a stranger on the street. Yet we find it quite reasonable to write about the fear of crime on the streets rather than about fear of automobile accidents, and a great many more people stay in the house at night for fear of crime than stay out of their cars for fear of accidents. Clearly, objective risk alone does not account for fear.

Several differences between motor vehicle risks and risks of victimization account for these differences in perception and fear. First, the risk of being the victim of a crime is highly concentrated in time and space. If one is walking on a downtown street at 2 A.M. by oneself, the risk is quite high. Walking at noon on a workday in the same place entails virtually no risk, just as it would be in many rural areas at any time of day or night. In contrast, the risk of automobile accidents is fairly constant. The holiday carnage on the highways is a few percentage points above the daily toll but, if divided by the volume of traffic, is probably not any higher at all. The risk rises somewhat if one drives during the evening hours, perhaps because more people are likely to have been drinking. However, most people do not know that driving is more dangerous in the evening hours. Therefore, a higher objective average risk is less feared because that risk does not come in intense periods that occupy the attention. Crime is more feared because there are certain times and places in which the risk is much higher. People who are hardly conscious of crime most of the time are occasionally sharply reminded by being in a fearful situation for a short time.

A second difference between the risk of automobile accidents and the risk of crime has to do with the presence of early signs of danger. Most of us have probably experienced an adrenalin reaction more often during the past year from a "close shave" in automobile traffic than from personal danger due to crime. That is, if we took a census of fear experiences during a year, we would probably find more fear experiences connected with automobiles than with crime. Ordinarily the fear experiences in automobiles happen to us when we had no reason whatever to expect an accident until the moment of the "close shave." We fear crime, however, in situations that give off danger signs in advance. The most elementary knowledge of crime rates makes one more afraid of a young man at night on the streets of the ghetto than of a young woman in early afternoon in a smalltown shopping plaza. Thus, fear requires not only periods and places of high risk but also recognition that we have entered a high-risk situation. That is, perception of risk depends both on the concentration of risk in time and space and on the presence of early signs of impending danger.

Once one perceives a high risk of damage or loss, there is still the question of whether one sees the potential damage as sufficiently serious to merit fear. This is what distinguishes violent street crime from crimes against property. For example, most of us know that, objectively, we are far more likely to have our bicycles stolen than to have money of equal value stolen from us at gunpoint. We take reasonable precautions with our bicycles (until we forget, or until we discover that the thieves carry bolt cutters), but we are not nearly as afraid of bicycle thieves as of robbers. When we go to societies in which people often leave their bicycles in racks without locking them (for instance, in the Netherlands), we find this to be a pleasant convenience. This is, however, quite different from the sense of relief that we feel when visiting an area in which we can walk freely at night. The reason is obviously that what we fear is not losing the $100 either for the bicycle or from the wallet—although we do not like this, of course—but having loaded guns waved in our faces.

Being threatened with a gun or a knife is frightening not because very many people get killed (though all too many do) but because the victim is suddenly confronted with a greatly increased chance of sudden death. Some robbers are nervous or crazy to begin with, and a victim can be injured or killed even if the robber did not initially intend it. When one is afraid, then, one is not only afraid of dying; one is also afraid of being held in a condition of being very afraid of dying. At any rate, it is the chance of death rather than the $100 loss that makes the experience fearful.

Thus far we have argued that a violent street crime like robbery is frightening because of the chance of death rather than because of property losses. To the chance of death during such an encounter, women must add the chance of rape. Here, too, the problem is primarily that as one is being raped one is being held in continuous fear of death. Because we cannot calculate the cost of rape as we can the cost of the stolen bicycle or wallet, rape is in some senses incomparable to robbery. A woman who has been raped can neither calculate nor recover her losses. Rape is also different from robbery because the fear of pain and chance of death are spread over a longer period of time. The acts of a man in an uncontrolled state are probably more likely to result in injury or death. Further, rapes probably take more time than robberies, so one experiences the fear of being killed over a longer period. The violent street encounter is thus doubly terrifying to a woman, because she also runs the risk of being raped, which is both more prolonged and more dangerous than being robbed. These factors may help to explain our earlier observation that women are more afraid of crime than men.

One can perceive that one is running a high risk of serious damage in some absolute sense and still feel that the risk is under one's control, and this sense of control somehow lessens one's fear. Motorcycles are much more dangerous than automobiles, but one does not have to drive a motorcycle. One may drink a bit too much at a party to be a safe driver, but one can be particularly careful. Steeplejacks and offshore oil drillers may have higher accident rates than other workers, but one can become a more skilled steeplejack or a more competent diver. Many of these efforts to control risk are magical—like the Trobriand Islanders' use of sacred canoes to keep them alive on the high seas—but they do help one resign oneself to the risk of substantial loss. Magic does not usually change people's view of the probability of loss; rather, it tends to make people feel they have done their best. The use of magical procedures thus transforms fear into a resigned acceptance of fate, which is psychologically more bearable than never having had a chance to do one's best. Earthquakes, mine disasters, train crashes, and crimes of violence all make people feel that their control over their fate is radically diminished. Similarly, the very fact that a crime is being committed implies that the criminal thinks the victim lacks the means to control the situation. In other high-risk situations, one can sometimes reduce either the amount of potential damage (by wearing a seatbelt in a car, for example) or the probability of damage or loss (by being a careful driver, for example). One can do a few things to avoid being the victim of a crime, but one cannot do very much to lessen the potential damage once one has been chosen as a victim. For all of these reasons, violent crime is greatly feared.

We have identified four components of the fear of crime: (1) the risks are concentrated in time and space; (2) there are early signs of risk that allow us to be afraid in advance; (3) there is serious potential damage involved; and (4) there is a sense of having no control over the risk. In the following sections, we will discuss ways to measure the various components of fear and will also present data about the distribution of the components of fear and of fear itself.

Measures and Components of Fear

According to the preceding discussion, the distribution of fear of crime should depend on the distributions of the four components of fear. We must therefore measure not just fear itself but also objective risk, perception of risk, vulnerability (or magnitude and seriousness of potential loss), and ability to control risk. Most of these components cannot be measured directly, but we can tap them indirectly through other factors that influence or are closely correlated with them.

In choosing variables to analyze the distribution of fear of crime, we will start with measures of objective risk. Risk is made up of hours of exposure to exceptionally dangerous situations. The character of the neighborhood one lives in and the number of hours during the day that one is alone, for example, affect one's exposure to high-risk situations. One's race also affects the danger one encounters, because black or integrated neighborhoods tend to be more dangerous than white ones. We will therefore use type of neighborhood (racially integrated or segregated—based on responses to a survey question about "blacks living nearby"), size of city, race, and living alone (without another adult) as measures of objective risk. Of course, these variables are only approximate measures of objective risk. One would expect that if the streets near one's house were dangerous, one would be more likely to be afraid. However, if one spends very little time on the street, the objective danger of street crime might have very little effect on one's level of fear.

The primary measures of vulnerability (or magnitude of potential loss) are difficult to separate from measures of whether people think they have any control over their own risks. One major correlate of vulnerability is sex: When the victim is female, there is both an added motive for criminal violence (that is, rape) and often less possibility for self-defense. Thus, sex is a measure of having more to lose, and also of one's ability to defend oneself. Other measures of vulnerability are similarly (though not so completely) confounded with measures of control over risk.

Measures of ability to reduce risk through self-defense include both personal characteristics and behavior. The most important personal characteristics are those predicting one's personal strength compared with that of young men (who commit most violent crimes). Age is such a characteristic for men but tends to be less important for women, because most women at all ages are weaker than young men. Thus we would expect an age-by-sex interaction predicting fear. Although we lack measures of most behavioral factors, we do have information about gun ownership; people who own guns may believe that they can do something about crime, even though they may not carry their guns on the streets.

In our previous discussion of perception of risk, we were primarily concerned with the determinants of perception. We argued that people were more likely to perceive risks when risks were concentrated in time and space and when danger signs gave early warnings of risk. We are now concerned with factors that distinguish between people rather than between sources of risk. Controlling for the source of risk, some people are more likely to perceive risk than others. One determinant of perception of risk is the experience of victimization: People who have been robbed are more likely to think that the risk of robbery is high, to be more sensitive to early signs of possible danger, to be more acutely aware that street crime can lead to serious injury or death, and to understand that victims often can neither prevent crime nor defend themselves against injury. Victimization experience should thus predict perception of risk and fear.

Violent crimes occur in many settings. Although a great many crimes of violence take place either at home or in bars in which people feel "at home," it is likely that most people do not equate "the crime problem" with the violent acts of their husbands, wives, or drinking buddies. Rather, the crime problem people fear is the problem of street crime. The question we use to measure fear of crime asks: "Is there any area right around here—that is within a mile—where you would be afraid to walk alone at night?" We recognize that the particular question people are given strongly shapes their responses. We cannot distinguish between perception of risk and the fear which that perception evokes. We are also unable to separate fear of various sorts of crime. In spite of these limitations, we can learn a great deal about the distribution of fear from our analysis of this question.

The Distribution of Objective Risk. Before we can study the distribution of fear, we need to know who it is that people *should* fear. Table 10 divides offenses into three main groups according to the social characteristics of people arrested for these offenses. The first group of crimes includes murder,

Table 10. Percentage of Males, Adult Males, and Blacks Arrested
for Various Offenses, 1975

Crime	Males[a]	Males over 18[b]	Blacks[b]
I. Crimes in which arrests are disproportionately adult black males			
Murder	88.4	75.9	55.3
Forcible rape	99.0	81.3	45.5
Aggravated assault	86.9	70.7	39.4
Weapons (carrying, possession)	92.0	76.1	41.5
Robbery	93.0	60.4	59.0
II. Crimes in which arrests are disproportionately juvenile males			
Burglary	94.6	44.3	28.4
Larceny, theft	68.8	35.2	30.6
Auto theft	93.0	42.0	26.5
III. Selected other offenses			
Drunkenness	92.9	89.9	19.3
Sex offenses other than rape and prostitution	92.3	73.5	19.4
Offenses against family and children	88.3	79.8	28.1
Other assaults (not aggravated)	86.2	69.4	33.6
Forgery, counterfeiting	71.1	61.9	32.4
Embezzlement and fraud	66.0	63.0	28.6
Prostitution and commercialized vice	25.7	24.6	53.2

Source: U.S. Bureau of the Census, 1976, Tables 272, 273, and 274.

[a]Based on people charged.

[b]Based on people arrested.

forcible rape, aggravated assault, carrying and possession of weapons, and robbery. The crimes in this group are not committed primarily by juveniles (though this is less true for robbery) but are all primarily crimes of adult males. Unlike the other crimes distinctive of adult males (including drunkenness and sex offenses other than rape or prostitution), the crimes in this group all show disproportionately high arrest rates for blacks—seven to eleven times the arrest rate of whites.

Crimes which the FBI considers serious but which lack the atmosphere of violence of crimes in the first group are disproportionately crimes of juvenile males. Burglary and auto theft, particularly, are heavily male crimes that are committed somewhere around fifteen to twenty times more frequently by juveniles than by other age groups. Larceny is also a crime of juveniles, though it is not quite so heavily male.

The offenses in the third group, except for prostitution, are male crimes in which juveniles and blacks are not noticeably overrepresented. (They are still disproportionately represented in most of these offenses, but not to the same degree as in groups I and II.) These are "ordinary white male adult crimes." Prostitution arrestees are disproportionately black women, but this probably reflects the fact that fewer white prostitutes for middle-class clients solicit on the street, where the risk of arrest is higher.

We call attention to these well-known statistics because they indicate the kind of people arrested for crimes that make people afraid. The crimes that frighten people most are just those crimes that are committed disproportionately by black adult males. Or, at the very least—since we do not know whether the relationship between crime and arrest is different for these crimes than for others—the fearful crimes are the ones which arrest information available to the public shows to be disproportionately adult black male crimes.

Victimization data by race also supports these inferences from the arrest distributions. The homicide rate among black people was about eight times as high as the white rate in 1974. According to the Census Bureau's victimization studies, reported robbery rates among black people are two or three times as high as among white people (U.S. Bureau of the Census, 1976, Tables 260 and 257). While the overall crime rate may or may not be higher among black people, crimes that make people afraid are more concentrated among black people. People who live near black people (mainly other black people) are also more likely to be victims of these crimes.

Table 11 shows the relationships between urbanism and the rates of certain serious offenses. We find that the most

Table 11. Urbanism Concentration Ratios by Offense, for Uniform Crime Reports "Serious Offenses," Crimes Known to the Police, 1975

	Offense						
	Category I. Black adult male crimes					Category II: Juvenile crimes	
Ratio	Robbery	Murder	Rape	Aggravated assault	Burglary	Larceny	Auto theft
Over ¼ million/ "Rural Area"	28.6	2.8	4.2	3.2	2.8	3.3	9.6
Over ¼ million/ "Suburban Area"	7.3	3.8	2.9	2.3	1.8	1.3	2.9
Over 1 million/ Over ¼ to ½ million "Suburban Area"/ "Rural Area"	1.9	1.4	1.1	1.3	.8	.7	1.3
	3.9	.7	1.5	1.4	1.6	2.5	3.3

Source: U.S. Bureau of the Census, 1976.

"urban" crime by all criteria is the violent street crime of robbery. All of the black adult male crimes are highly concentrated in the central cities of large metropolitan areas. Robbery is especially concentrated in the very largest of these metropolitan central cities. Fear-producing crimes occur disproportionately in large cities, disproportionately victimize black people, and disproportionately produce arrests of adult black males. Or, to put it more succinctly, the most fear-producing crimes are all "ghetto crimes."

The pattern of violent crimes being disproportionately ghetto crimes has become more marked in recent years: The rise in violent crime has been disproportionately a rise in ghetto crime, so violence is more concentrated in the ghetto now than it was fifteen years ago. The ghetto concentration of violent crimes does seem to have been decreasing lately, though. We will discuss these changes in greater detail later in this section.

The percentages of people arrested for three major street crimes who were black in 1961, 1971, and 1975 were:

	1961	1971	1975
Robbery	48.5	66.4	59.0
Murder	52.2	62.4	55.3
Rape	41.2	50.3	45.5

In the 1960s, then, there was a sharp increase on the order of 10 to 20 percent in the percentage of blacks arrested for the three major violent crimes. A partial recession in percentages of black arrests occurred in the first part of the 1970s. Proportionately, the black arrest rate for robbery in 1961 was about seven times the white rate; it increased to about fifteen times the white rate in 1971, then decreased to about ten times the white rate in 1975. The doubling of the black rate relative to the white rate during the 1960s indicates an increasing concentration of dangerous crime in the ghetto.

The same increasing concentration of violent crime in the ghetto during the 1960s shows up in the statistics on concentration of crimes in cities. During the twelve years between 1962 and 1974, the robbery rate in the big cities grew by 411 percent; the robbery rate in rural areas grew by "only" 212 percent. This means that, although in 1962 people living in big cities were already 14.7 times as likely to be robbed as rural people, their vulnerability grew twice as fast in the twelve succeeding years: By 1974, city dwellers were 28.6 times as vulnerable to robbery as rural people were.

The public facts of the matter are that the big city ghetto is a very dangerous place and that it has been getting differentially more dangerous. Nonviolent crimes like embezzlement or fraud are not very concentrated in the ghetto and are not becoming more concentrated there. But if the rate of urban robbery continues to grow in cities with over a quarter of a million people at the same rate as it grew from 1962 to 1974, by the year 2024 each man, woman, and child in a large city would be robbed by force or threat of force 2.3 times per year. Further, because children are rarely victims of robbery and females are robbed less frequently than men, an average male in the year 2024 might expect to be robbed once a month. There are all sorts of reasons not to trust this projection. In particular, the concentration of crime in the big cities has started to decrease recently. Still, fear of the large urban ghetto ought to have been growing over the past fifteen years and ought to be manifested in our survey data from the 1970s. We would expect to find this urban/rural difference reflected both in the patterns of reports of victimization and in the patterns of fear of walking the streets at night.

We have cited FBI arrest statistics and census victimization data to show that the most violent crimes are committed primarily by black adult males in the big cities. Our data from the General Social Survey confirm these findings. Table 12 gives the percentages of respondents who said they had been burglarized or robbed during the preceding year. (The questions asked in the General Social Survey are ordered in a different way than in the victimization studies reported on by the U.S. Bureau of the Census [1976] and give a higher rate.) The incidence of burglary is 1.2 times more frequent for whites living near black people than for whites living in segregated neighborhoods. Further, it is about twice as frequent for whites

Table 12. Victimization Rates by Type of Neighborhood

Race and neighborhood	City Size			
	Less than 10,000	10,000 to 250,000	250,000 or more	All sizes
Whites in segregated white neighborhoods				
Burglary	4.6 (1479)[a]	6.4 (1211)	8.7 (264)	5.7 (2954)
Robbery	.8 (1470)	1.5 (1207)	2.7 (264)	1.3 (2941)
Whites in integrated neighborhoods				
Burglary	5.3 (606)	8.3 (1013)	10.7 (540)	8.1 (2159)
Robbery	1.5 (606)	1.9 (1013)	5.9 (540)	2.8 (2159)
Blacks in all kinds of neighborhoods				
Burglary				10.5 (660)
Robbery				3.9 (653)

Source: General Social Surveys, 1973-1974 and 1976-1977 combined.
[a]Raw frequencies indicated in parentheses.

living in cities with over a quarter of a million people than for whites living in smaller cities or rural areas. The burglary rate for whites living in large cities near black people is over twice as high as the rate for whites living in segregated neighborhoods in more sparsely populated areas. Similarly, white people report being robbed about 1.7 times as often if they live near blacks than if they live in segregated neighborhoods, and the robbery rate for whites in the largest cities is nearly four times the corresponding robbery rate in less densely populated areas. Thus, a white person is about six times as likely to be robbed if he or she lives near a typical ghetto. The concentration of these crimes in the ghetto is further confirmed by the black victimization rates. For burglary the black victimization rate (not broken down by size of city) is about the same as the victimization rates for whites living near blacks in big cities; for robbery the white rate is a little higher than the overall black rate. Of interest in this regard is that although blacks are more likely than whites to live in the largest cities, more than half of the black population lives in the two smaller size classifications.

Victimization also varies with the type of household in which a respondent lives—in particular, whether or not another adult lives in the household. Of the 408 respondents in the 1973 and 1974 General Social Surveys living in single-adult households, 11.8 percent reported having been burglarized. This is nearly twice the 6.9 percent burglary rate of the 2,548 people who lived with another adult. This ratio of double victimization for people who live alone (or at least without other adults) holds also for robbery: Among the 408 respondents who lived alone, 4.4 percent reported a robbery within the previous year, while only 2.2 percent of the 2,537 respondents who lived with another adult reported a robbery.

Objective Risk and Fear. In the preceding section, we found that victimization varies with the type of neighborhood in which one lives and with the composition of one's household. We also argued that violent street crime is the sort of crime that makes people afraid. Given this information, we would expect to find that the distribution of fear is quite similar to the distribution of victimization (see Biderman and others, 1967; Furstenberg, 1971). That is, we would expect to find that adults who live alone are more afraid than those who live with other adults and that people who live in integrated neighborhoods in big cities are more afraid than those who live in segregated neighborhoods in small towns or rural areas.

In Table 13 we report the impact of these three determinants of objective risk (city size, racial composition of the neighborhood, and household composition) on fear of walking at night in one's neighborhood. In all cases, people are more afraid in larger cities. In all but one comparison, people who live alone are significantly more likely to be afraid. (In the integrated neighborhoods of the largest cities, whites who live alone are no more fearful than those who live with another adult.) In all comparisons but two, whites who live in integrated neighborhoods are significantly more afraid of the streets of their neighborhoods than whites who live in all-white neighborhoods. (The two exceptions to this trend are people who live alone in middle and very large cities.) Black people are more afraid of crime than are whites (except whites who live in integrated neighborhoods of medium or large cities). In the aggregate, then, blacks are a good deal more afraid of crime than whites. If there were enough cases to analyze subgroups of the black population reliably, we would learn that blacks are also more fearful *within* any category of city size. The broad pattern of fear therefore corresponds to the broad pattern of victimization: The nearer one lives to the ghetto and the more alone one is, the more one lives (or at least walks) in fear.

Sex and Fear. Earlier in this chapter we argued that fear was related to the seriousness of the potential injury or loss (vulnerability) as well as to the probability of victimization (objective risk). Our main measure of vulnerability is sex. Women have more to lose in a violent encounter. If women and men spent approximately equal amounts of time on the street and were about equally likely to be robbed or assaulted, we would still expect women to be more afraid than men because they are more vulnerable than men. In fact, women are robbed, assaulted, and murdered less frequently than men; however,

Table 13. Percentage of People Afraid, by Neighborhood Type and Living with
Another Adult for Whites, and by Living with Another Adult for Blacks (Percentage Afraid)

Racial composition of neighborhood and household composition	City Size			
	Less than 10,000	10,000 to 250,000	250,000 or more	All sizes
Whites by type of neighborhood and household composition				
Segregated white				
with another adult	27.2 (1294)[a]	40.0 (1017)	47.6 (208)	34.1 (2519)
Alone	35.6 (180)	57.7 (189)	66.0 (53)	49.3 (422)
Integrated				
with another adult	32.8 (537)	48.3 (837)	67.9 (380)	47.8 (1754)
Alone	41.2 (68)	59.4 (170)	68.6 (153)	57.8 (391)
Blacks in all neighborhoods, by household composition				
With another adult				55.4 (466)
Alone				62.4 (186)

Source: General Social Surveys, 1973-1974 and 1976-1977 combined.
[a] Raw frequencies indicated in parentheses.

almost all rape victims are women. Robbery and assault are thus likely to be more frightening experiences for women than for men, and we would expect women to be more afraid than men in similar circumstances.

We have seen that the percentage of people who are afraid to walk in their neighborhoods rises from about one quarter in segregated small towns to over one half in or near the ghetto. We have also seen that fear is greater among those who have higher risks because they live alone. These findings indicate that fear is related to risk. Now we will examine our data to see if fear is also related to vulnerability.

Table 14 shows that in all categories of objective risk, women are much more likely than men to be afraid of the streets in their neighborhoods. The weighted estimate of the average percentage difference by sex within neighborhood and living situation is 38 percent. Controlling for sex decreases the difference in fear due to living situation. Women are more likely to live alone, and women are much more likely to be afraid; therefore, part of the relationship between living alone and fear is due not to the higher risks of those who live alone but to the higher vulnerability of women, who more often live alone. The average difference in percentage afraid by living situation, controlling for sex and neighborhood type, is 6.1 percent.

Age and Fear. As we mentioned earlier, sex as a measure of vulnerability is confounded with sex as a measure of one's sense of control over risk. While it seems perfectly reasonable to argue that women are more afraid than men because they have more to lose, we must keep in mind that it would be equally plausible to argue that women are more afraid because they can do less to defend themselves. That is, if we think of sex as a measure of efficacy, or ability to control or reduce risk, then the relation between sex and fear of crime is due to women's inability to defend themselves. Our data on the relation between sex and fear do not help us distinguish between these two possible explanations or tell us which of the two is more important if both hold.

If we want to explore the relation between efficacy and

Table 14. Impact of Sex on Fear, by Neighborhood Type (Condensed) and Household Composition (Percentage Afraid)

Race and neighborhood	Males		Females	
	Living with another adult	Living Alone	Living with another adult	Living Alone
Whites in small cities and rural	10.1 (891)[a]	5.4 (92)	46.6 (940)	55.8 (156)
Whites in segregated large and medium cities	21.9 (593)	34.8 (69)	59.5 (632)	69.4 (173)
Whites in integrated large and medium cities	33.3 (577)	44.3 (140)	73.4 (640)	78.7 (183)
Blacks in all neighborhoods	36.5 (222)	41.3 (63)	72.5 (244)	73.2 (123)

Source: General Social Surveys, 1973-1974 and 1976-1977 combined.

[a]Raw frequencies indicated in parentheses.

fear, then, we must look for another measure of efficacy, and one measure of helplessness in the face of violence is age. Generally speaking, strength and speed (and perhaps the willingness to look ridiculous by running away) decrease with age. The relative disadvantage compared with the young adult men who commit most of the violent crimes is already great for most women, though. Thus the principal effect of age on the person's imagined capacity to do something about the risks of street crime (in other words, the principal impact of age on the sense of efficacy) should occur among men. We would predict, then, that age would have very little effect on fear among women, but that older men would be more afraid than younger men. Only in old age would men begin to experience the defensive disadvantage which women experience all their lives. However, if the higher vulnerability of women explains part of their greater fear, then even older men should be less afraid than women.

Table 15 shows that these inferences are approximately right. Older women are a little more afraid than all women

Table 15. Impact of Age and Sex on Fear (Percentage Afraid)

| | Sex | |
Age	Male	Female
Young (18-29)	18.8 (713)[a]	61.1 (795)
Adult (30-44)	17.6 (709)	57.9 (933)
Mature (45-59)	22.0 (669)	61.0 (777)
Old (60 and over)	33.1 (647)	68.2 (729)

Source: General Social Surveys, 1973, 1974, 1976 and 1977.

[a]Raw frequencies indicated in parentheses.

younger than 59. This difference, when corrected for cluster sampling, is significant at the .05 level. The effect looks larger among men: The percentage difference between old and young is 14.3 for men but only 7.1 for women. However, this difference is significant by random sampling standards but non-significant when a correction is made for cluster sampling. (Age and sex are not very clustered, so perhaps no correction is necessary). All we can say for sure is that the data support the hypothesis that age makes more difference in fear for men than it does for women. More to the point, though, is that age, like sex, influences fear among those who are weaker relative to young adult males. Differences in efficacy are not sufficient to explain the difference in fear between the sexes, however, because even the most efficacious women (young) are more afraid than the most inefficacious men (old) and because age has little effect on fear among women.

Gun Ownership and Fear. A third measure of efficacy is gun ownership. People who own guns may imagine that they can do something about violence, and they may therefore be less afraid to walk near their houses at night. Table 16 shows the relationship among whites between gun ownership and being afraid, controlling for sex. In all cases, gun owners are less fearful than nonowners; among both males and females, this

Table 16. **Fear of Walking Alone in Neighborhood for Whites, by Gun Ownership and Sex (Percentage Afraid)**

Sex	Gun Ownership	
	Own Gun	*No Gun*
Males	17.1 (1320)[a]	25.7 (1081)
Females	55.9 (1285)	64.1 (1531)

Source: General Social Surveys, 1973-1974 and 1976-1977 combined.

[a]Raw frequencies indicated in parentheses.

difference is about 9 percent. It is clear, then, that people who have guns are less likely to be afraid to walk around the neighborhood at night. This connection between behavior and fear is peculiar, though, because people do not ordinarily carry their guns with them when they walk around at night. The question on gun ownership asks about guns in the household. Because women are more likely to live alone than are men, and because men are the owners of most guns, women are about 10 percent less likely to report that they have guns in the household. We know that women are more likely to be afraid than men, so part of the relationship between gun ownership and fear might be due to sex. But we have already controlled for sex in Table 16, and there is still about a 9 percent difference in fear between those who own guns and those who do not.

However there is also a very strong relationship between gun ownership and living near the ghetto. Table 17 shows that in all city sizes, white people who live nearer to black people are less likely to have guns and whites who live in larger cities are also less likely to own guns. The rate of gun ownership for white families living in large central cities near black people is about half the rate for white families living in segregated small towns and rural areas. Fear is much more frequent in large cities and in neighborhoods near the ghetto, so a spurious relationship is created between fear and gun ownership. Similarly, black people, who are much more likely to be afraid of the streets near their homes, are also much less likely to own guns.

When these forces are combined, they are almost sufficient to explain the apparent relation between gun ownership and fear as shown in Table 18. Within neighborhood type and sex, there is no significant relationship between gun ownership and fear of walking about in the neighborhood for women, and only a very small relationship for men (the weighted average difference in fear among men is 2.4 percent).

In the preceding sections we have discussed the relationship between fear and three measures of efficacy, or ability to control or reduce risk. Sex, the first measure of efficacy, is also a measure of vulnerability. This means that we cannot determine how much of the relation between fear and sex is due to the fact that women are more vulnerable than men and how much is due to the fact that women are less able to defend themselves. Age, the second measure of efficacy, has a small relationship to fear among women and a much larger one among men. The relationship between gun ownership, the third measure of efficacy, and fear is mostly spurious. We can thus conclude that a sense of control does in fact tend to make one less afraid of walking on the streets of one's neighborhood. Perhaps if we had better measures of efficacy—such as general physical condition, physical prowess, self-defense training, and a personal presence that conveys the message, "Don't mess with me "—we might find a stronger relation between fear and ability to control risk.

Victimization and Fear. In the theory outlined in the

Table 17. Gun Ownership by Sex, Neighborhood Type, and Race (Percentage Owning Guns)

Racial composition of neighborhood and sex	Race and city size				
	Whites			Blacks	
	Less than 10,000	10,000 to 250,000	250,000 or more	250,000 or more	All neighborhoods
Males					
Segregated	71.6 (682)[a]	51.3 (540)	26.0 (123)		40.5 (284)
Integrated	66.0 (300)	46.0 (472)	31.6 (247)		
Females					
Segregated	64.2 (795)	41.6 (669)	25.2 (139)		32.2 (370)
Integrated	54.9 (306)	33.0 (537)	26.2 (290)		

Source: General Social Surveys, 1973-1974 and 1976-1977 combined.
[a] Raw frequencies indicated in parentheses.

Table 18. Fear and Gun Ownership, Controlling Sex, Race, and Neighborhood Type (Percentage Afraid)

Sex, racial composition of neighborhood, and gun ownership	Race and city size			
	Whites		Blacks	All
	Less than 10,000	10,000 to 250,000	250,000 or more	neighborhoods
Males				
Segregated white				
Own Gun	7.4 (488)[a]	20.4 (275)	31.3 (32)	
No Gun	11.1 (189)	20.1 (254)	38.9 (90)	
Integrated				
Own Gun	11.1 (198)	27.1 (221)	50.0 (78)	35.7 (115)
No Gun	13.4 (97)	29.7 (246)	49.1 (167)	39.4 (165)
Females				
Segregated white				
Own Gun	43.1 (508)	61.5 (278)	70.6 (34)	
No Gun	50.5 (277)	60.3 (380)	63.7 (102)	
Integrated				
Own Gun	55.4 (168)	65.5 (174)	88.2 (76)	76.1 (117)
No Gun	53.8 (132)	71.0 (355)	82.9 (210)	70.9 (247)

Source: General Social Surveys 1973, 1974, 1976 and 1977 combined.

Note: The average difference (unweighted) for fear for males is 2.7 percent, with males in no-gun households being more afraid. For females, the average difference in fear is 1.0 percent (essentially no difference), with women in gun-owning households being more afraid.

[a]Raw frequencies indicated in parentheses.

introductory pages of this chapter, people are imagined to act rather like insurance companies, coldly calculating the odds of risk. But some insurance companies adjust the premiums on automobile insurance when one has an accident; so also, evidently, people change their perceptions of their risks (or realize more vividly how much they have at stake) when they experience victimization. The experience of victimization may tend to make people more sensitive to the cues that precede danger, to their own defenselessness, and so forth, thus forcing them to reassess their estimates of the danger of particular situations. Because the perception of high risk, vulnerability, and inefficacy make people afraid, the experience of victimization should affect fear, as it affects these intermediate variables.

Table 19 shows the effect of the experience of victimization on fear of walking in the neighborhood, controlling for the type of neighborhood (and hence controlling in part for the objective risks). People who have been robbed are about 23 percent more likely to be afraid than other people who live in the same sorts of neighborhoods. Comparing robbery with burglary, we find that the experience of robbery, a crime disproportionately committed by adults and by threat with weapons, has a far greater effect on fear than does the crime of burglary, which is committed much more often by juveniles and generally does not involve weapons. There is roughly a 9 percent difference in fear produced by the experience of being burglarized during the past year compared with the 23 percent difference for robbery. Thus we can conclude that victimization affects one's perception of danger and therefore makes one more afraid. (Biderman and others, 1967, reach the opposite conclusion using data from studies on Washington, D.C.)

The Rationality of Fear of the Streets. The broad patterns of response to the fear question suggest that people estimate their risks and the amount of damage that might be done to them fairly accurately: People in more dangerous neighborhoods are more afraid of their streets. If we assume that blacks live in the same kinds of neighborhoods as whites who live near blacks, the two races make quite similar estimates of the dangers of the same neighborhoods, even though the danger (according

Table 19. Fear, Neighborhood Type (Condensed), and Victimization Experience (Percentage Afraid)

	Race and neighborhood type			
	Whites		Blacks	
Victimization Experience	Small and rural	Segregated white large and medium	Integrated large and medium	All neighborhoods
Not robbed	29.7 (2050)[a]	44.1 (1438)	55.4 (1492)	56.8 (618)
Robbed	52.4 (21)	56.0 (25)	84.0 (50)	72.4 (29)
Not burglarized	29.8 (1979)	43.6 (1365)	55.6 (1402)	55.6 (579)
Burglarized	33.0 (100)	53.5 (101)	63.6 (140)	70.7 (75)

Source: General Social Surveys, 1973-1974 and 1976-1977 combined.

[a] Raw frequencies indicated in parentheses.

to the arrest statistics) falls disproportionately to blacks. Women are more afraid than men, and this seems to be due to a combination of two sensible reasons: First, women are more likely to be raped and are therefore more vulnerable than men. Second, women are weaker (or at least believe they are weaker) than the people who ordinarily commit violent crimes. Further evidence that weakness is a relevant variable comes from the impact of age on fear. We would expect age to have a greater effect on fear among men than among women, because age has a greater effect on strength relative to potential criminals for men than for women. This does seem to be the case, though the relationship is not very strong.

The preliminary evidence that owning a gun made people feel more comfortable on the streets (where presumably they do not carry guns) suggested an element of "magic" in people's perceptions of what they can do about crimes of violence. But when the figures were controlled for the fact that women and large-city residents do not own guns as often as rural males, it turned out that gun ownership had very little influence on fear. It is not a magical belief in guns that makes gun owners less afraid but rather the fact that gun owners are men who live in rural areas, where risks are low.

We also found that people who have been robbed or burglarized are much more fearful than those who have not been victimized. This response—especially the drastic change in the level of fear among people who have been robbed—is the nearest thing we have found to a "gut reaction." There are two possible explanations for this increase in fear—one rational and the other nonrational. Concerning the rational response, we found that the experience of being robbed or burglarized leads to a reassessment of risk, vulnerability, and efficacy. The higher levels of fear of those who have been victimized can then be interpreted in two ways: Either the victims are similar to nonvictims except that they now have a more realistic assessment of the danger of nighttime streets, or the victims are actually more vulnerable and inefficacious than their peers living in "similar" neighborhoods, and their higher levels of fear reflect this objective difference. However, if we are to explain the differences in fear between those who have been robbed and those who have not, we must be able to find large differences between victims and "similar" nonvictims or else we must assume that nonvictims make very bad estimates of danger. Both of these assumptions are somewhat implausible, so we now suggest that our explanation should also include non-rational responses: that is, at least part of the increase in fear among robbery victims is due to a gut reaction rather than to a cool reassessment of risk, vulnerability, and efficacy. This increase in fear might be related to the psychological effects of having faced the possiblilty of a violent death.

In fact, we find that one traditional form of irrationality —racial prejudice—*is* related to fear: Table 20 shows that people

Table 20. Relation of Whites' Fear of Neighborhood to Race Prejudice,[a] by Sex and Living Near Blacks (Percentage Afraid)

	Distance to blacks	
Sex and prejudice	Close	Far
Males, unprejudiced	26.7 (682)[b]	14.4 (687)
Males, prejudiced	32.6 (341)	17.1 (655)
Females, unprejudiced	67.7 (737)	47.3 (789)
Females, prejudiced	72.0 (396)	59.8 (803)

Source: General Social Surveys, 1973-1974 and 1976-1977 combined.

[a]"Race Prejudice" was measured with three items on race relations that occurred on the four surveys with the fear question: approval of laws against interracial marriage, objection to someone in the family bringing a black person home to dinner, and whether or not anyone in the family has actually brought a black person home for dinner. The scale was then divided to yield a split approximately at the median. "Unprejudiced" people gave unprejudiced answers to at least two of these questions. The differences between prejudiced and unprejudiced males who live close to blacks is significant, and the difference for females who live far from blacks is significant. Overall the controlled difference between prejudiced and unprejudiced people is significant.

[b]Raw frequencies indicated in parentheses.

who score high on a scale of racial prejudice are more afraid of crime than people who are more liberal on race relations. (see Furstenberg, 1971). One might suspect that this is related to the problem of the high concentration of blacks among arrestees for violent crimes. However there is just as much relation between racial prejudice and fear of walking in one's neighborhood in segregated areas as in neighborhoods where the real danger might come disproportionately from blacks. That is, the relationship between racial prejudice and fear is not due to sharpened perception of the truth about crime; rather, the relation is due to the fact that racial prejudice is part of a general tendency to fear the unknown. This tendency causes people to fear those unknown others whom they encounter when walking about at night as well as black people whom they are not likely to know well (see Conklin, 1971; McIntyre, 1967; President's Commission on Law Enforcement and the Administration of Justice, 1967).

We have been analyzing data on a particular question about fear—namely fear of the streets of one's neighborhood at night—but we have excluded such sources of continuous fear as a husband who becomes violent when he gets drunk or a young man who has convinced himself that resistance to his sexual advances is actually intended to encourage him. We also have not explored the type of anxiety that results when the person who is going to drive one home after a party has drunk too much, but not quite enough so that one can politely insist on driving oneself. Many people are not as afraid of crime as of cancer, but many more years of life are taken by cancer than by young adult males in the ghetto. In spite of the limitations of our analysis, however, fear of crime is an important component of one's satisfaction with the community and probably has a great effect on the way neighbors relate to each other.

Now that we have examined the relationship between crime and fear, we can turn to the relationship between fear and punitiveness. Punitiveness is obviously an attempt to deal with the crime problem. We punish criminals partly because we think criminals deserve to suffer for their wrongdoings but primarily because we think that punishment will somehow reduce crime. Thus we hypothesize that the relationship between fear and punitiveness is a fairly straightforward one: When crime is salient, people will give more punitive responses to survey questions. If fear is a measure of salience of the crime problem, then we could expect that fearful people would tend to favor capital punishment and harsh courts.

We can test the hypothesis that salience of crime leads to punitiveness in a second way. Recognizing that salience may be too complex to measure with the question on fear, we also argue that crime may be salient to some respondents who are not afraid, either because they live in safe areas or for other reasons. An alternative measure of the salience of crime is provided by the question about the most important national problem. We therefore examine the relationship between punitive attitudes and the belief that a social control problem is the nation's most pressing problem.

Fear and Social Control Attitudes

If people develop punitive attitudes because of fear of crime, then we should find that people who are more afraid are more punitive. We already know that certain subgroups simply do not fit this pattern: In general, black people are more afraid than whites but not more punitive; in general, southerners are less afraid than northerners but not less punitive; and women are generally much more afraid than men and somewhat less punitive. That is, factors that generally cause fear (or for other reasons are associated with fear) do not generally cause punitive attitudes. Nevertheless, this issue is worth investigating because in recent years people have become both more fearful of crime and more punitive.

The first part of Table 21 shows the relationship for whites between fear of walking alone at night and wanting harsher courts in 1965. When we control for sex, fearful people are about 16.0 percent more punitive than people who are not afraid. Thus, in 1965 the individual-level cross-tabulation would lead us to predict that, in general, the public would become more punitive as the level of fear increased and, more specifically, that women would be more punitive than men, blacks more punitive than whites, northerners more punitive than southerners, and city dwellers more punitive than rural people.

Table 21. Assessments of Harshness of Local Courts, Fear of Walking
Alone at Night in the Neighborhood, and Sex of the Respondent
(Whites Only) (Percentage Who Think the Courts are Not Harsh Enough)

Sex and year	Fear	
	Afraid	Not Afraid
1965:		
Males	74.7 (99)[a]	59.2 (480)
Females	61.5 (286)	45.2 (283)
1973-1974:		
Males	86.0 (172)	81.3 (675)
Females	84.4 (550)	80.8 (380)
1976-1977:		
Males	92.1 (252)	85.7 (897)
Females	88.3 (853)	86.3 (532)

Source: Gallup survey, 1965; General Social Surveys, 1973-1974 combined,
1976-1977 combined.

[a]Raw frequencies indicated in parentheses.

The second and third parts of Table 21 report the same
relationships in 1973-1974 and 1976-1977, respectively. Both
show that we were well advised to be suspicious of this relationship. The weighted average difference in punitiveness for the
two sexes is 4.1 percent in 1973-1974 and 4.0 percent in 1976-
1977, with more fearful people being only slightly more punitive
than less fearful ones. (Both of these differences are significant
by random sampling standards but probably not significant
when we correct for cluster sampling. Taken together, they
show there probably is a small relation between fear and punitiveness.) This time there is not much of a sex difference to
reduce this relationship between fear and punitiveness. Women
are only about 1.0 percent less punitive than men when we
control for fear; this is not statistically significant. That is,
there is neither a strong relationship between fear and punitiveness nor a strong relationship between sex and punitiveness.

If the relationship between fear and punitiveness in 1965
is combined with the increase in fear that we observed between
1965 and 1973-1974 (33.5 percent were afraid in 1965 while
40.6 percent were afraid in 1973-1974), we would have predicted that punitiveness would increase 1.1 percent (16.0
percent difference in punitiveness by level of fear times 7.1

percent increase in fear). Instead, we have to explain a difference of 19.4 percent, because 49.0 percent wanted harsher courts in 1965 compared with 68.4 percent in 1973-1974. Clearly the relationship between fear and punitiveness (as measured by the courts question) and the increase in fear are not much help in explaining this large increase in punitiveness.

Unfortunately, we cannot use attitudes toward capital punishment, our second measure of punitiveness, to verify this change in the relation between fear and punitiveness, because we do not have the two relevant questions on the same survey. The data for measuring the relationship between fear and support for capital punishment are only available in the 1970s. Table 22 tabulates capital punishment attitudes by level of fear

Table 22. Attitudes Toward Capital Punishment, Fear of Walking Alone at Night in the Neighborhood, and Sex of the Respondent (Whites Only; Percentage Favoring Capital Punishment)

Sex and year	Fear	
	Afraid	Not afraid
1973-1974:		
Males	72.9 (240)[a]	73.7 (946)
Females	66.4 (758)	59.8 (515)
1976-1977:		
Males	82.0 (256)	78.5 (907)
Females	70.4 (831)	63.4 (536)

Source: General Social Surveys, 1973-74 combined and 1976-77 combined.
[a]Raw frequencies indicated in parentheses.

in 1973-1974 and in 1976-1977. When we control for sex, we find that people who are afraid are about 3.5 percent more punitive than those who are not afraid in 1973-1974 and 5.3 percent more in 1976-1977. This difference in attitudes toward capital punishment is of the same order of magnitude as the difference in attitudes toward the courts in the 1970s, though it seems that the relationship between fear and favoring capital punishment is stronger among women than among men.

We have found that the relationship between fear and punitiveness has not been constant over time. Though there was a strong connection in 1965 between an individual respondent's fear of crime and his or her punitive attitudes, this connection has become much weaker in the 1970s. We do not know whether capital punishment attitudes were related to fear in the 1960s, but we do know that more fearful people did want the courts to deal more harshly with criminals. In the 1970s, a respondent's own fear is no longer related to punitive attitudes, yet a more fearful society is also a more punitive society. Even if the 1960s relation between fear and punitiveness had persisted into the 1970s, we still could not have explained much of the increase in punitiveness—the relation between fear and punitiveness and the increase in fear were simply not large enough. But the weakening of this association means that the increase in fear explains essentially none of the increase in punitiveness. We must, therefore, look elsewhere if we want to account for the punitiveness of the 1970s.

Social Control Problems and Punitiveness

Fear of walking alone in one's neighborhood is a measure of what might be called "personal salience of crime." We have shown in Chapter Two that at the same time that fear of crime was increasing, the percentage of people who named some social control problem as the nation's most important problem was increasing. This might be called "public salience of crime." People who are not afraid in their own neighborhoods might well think that crime in general is an important public problem and might sympathize with people who live in neighborhoods in which they would be afraid. Perhaps the punitiveness of the 1970s can be explained by an increase in the "public salience of crime." (Furstenberg, 1971, obtained data suggesting that these two measures of salience are almost unrelated.)

Three Gallup surveys include both the question on harsher courts and the question about the nation's "most important problem." In Table 23, we classify respondents according to whether they mentioned some social control problem as the most important problem, and we give the percentage favoring harsher courts in each category. In all three years, the percentages wanting courts to be harsher are larger among those seeing

Table 23. Assessments of Harshness of Local Courts and
Most Important National Problem (Percentage Who Think the Courts
Are Not Harsh Enough)

	Most important problem	
Year	Social control	Other problems
1965	55.2 (625)[a]	48.6 (3726)
1968	71.9 (302)	60.7 (1375)
1969	78.2 (344)	73.2 (1267)

Source: Gallup Polls March 1965, January 1968, and January 1969.

[a]Raw frequencies indicated in parentheses.

social control as the most important problem, though in 1969
the difference is barely significant (and is not significant if we
take into account the clustering effect of the multi-stage sampling). Even though the relationship taken as a whole is statistically significant, it is not large enough to argue that the
increasing salience of crime as a public problem explains the
increase in punitiveness over the four years.

Table 24 reports the results from two Gallup Polls that
included the item on capital punishment along with the most

Table 24. Attitudes Toward Capital Punishment and Most
Important National Problem (Percentage Favoring Capital Punishment)

	Most important problem	
Year	Social control	Other problems
1957	57.1 (70)[a]	58.2 (1177)
1971	59.6 (567)	51.9 (931)

Source: Gallup Polls, 1957 and 1971.

[a]Raw frequencies indicated in parentheses.

important problem question. In 1957 there were so few people
(only 5.6 percent) who mentioned social control problems
(such as crime, delinquency, and safety) as the most important
national problem that the percentage favoring capital punishment is fairly unreliable. There is no evidence that, at that
time, people who thought crime was the most important problem
were any more punitive toward murderers than were people
who thought other problems were more important than social
control. By 1971, a much larger percentage (37.9 percent)

named social control problems as the most important national problem. Further, those who say social control is the nation's most important problem are more likely by 7.7 percent to favor capital punishment than those who choose some other problem.

Overall these results show that salience of crime in the public domain has about the same positive but weak effect on punitiveness as does salience of crime in the private domain. Thinking crime is an important national problem and thinking crime is a problem on the streets of one's own neighborhood have about the same impact on one's attitudes toward social control. In both cases, the effects at the individual level are small, and in neither case can we explain the surge in punitiveness by the salience of crime measured at the individual level.

Summary

We have explored various aspects of mass psychology that might explain fear of crime and connect the recent history of the fear of crime to punitive attitudes. Figure 1 illustrates our findings schematically. We found that fear of crime is a perfectly sensible response: People are more afraid of crime when they are more exposed to it, when the damages they might sustain are larger, or when they have fewer resources to protect themselves. Except for the impact of racial prejudice on fear (which, incidentally, is about the same size as the impact of racial prejudice on punitiveness), there is little doubt about why people are afraid of the streets of their neighborhoods.

Most of the obvious connections that one would have expected to find between salience of crime and punitiveness are in fact there, though they are quite weak. Punitive attitudes are in part a reaction to the personal and public salience of crime. Individuals who are themselves more afraid or who think crime is an important national problem are more likely to be punitive. This relationship may have been stronger in the past —especially for the courts question, which produces less moral resistance to becoming more punitive. It is apparently much easier to favor longer prison sentences for the average serious crime arrest than to favor capital punishment for murderers.

Figure 1. Interrelationship of Variables in Chapter Three

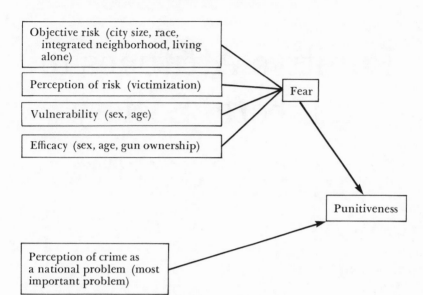

Overall, then, we can say that though the increased salience of crime at an individual level does increase punitiveness, this increase is not large enough to account for the general upward trend in the level of punitiveness in public opinion.

Though we have succeeded reasonably well in explaining fear of crime, we have not succeeded in providing an explanation of the recent drastic changes in the level of punitiveness. From the evidence in this chapter, these increases in punitiveness seem to have something to do with the increased salience of crime, both as manifested at the personal level in the increases in fear and manifested at the collective level of increased mentions of crime as the nation's most important problem.

4

Punitive Attitudes in a Liberal Society

The central issue of this chapter is the relationship between liberalism and punitiveness. The empirical puzzle is that while liberal attitudes toward race relations, civil liberties, abortion, and sex roles were increasing by about 1 to 1.5 percent per year since the middle 1950s, punitive responses were moving in the opposite direction. This puzzle is intensified by the results of Chapter Three which show that the increase in fear of crime has not been substantial enough to offset a tendency toward lenience caused by general liberalization; in fact, the increase in fear of crime is not even substantial enough to explain the increase in punitiveness in the absence of liberalizing trends.

In order to penetrate this puzzle further we will examine why the tradition of American liberalism leads to lenient opinions on the treatment of criminals. Only if we understand the cross-sectional correlation between liberalism and lenience can we explain why recent increases in liberalism do not lead to increases in lenience. Because we are asking people about a public policy toward criminals—rather than for their angry

74

reactions to being victimized—we must explore the determinants of whether people think the punishments dealt out by
public authorities are fair or not.

The Components of Fair Punishment

For a punishment to be considered fair, most people require that the person punished be guilty of the offense for
which he or she is being punished, that the punishment be
appropriate to the crime, and that the punishment be (more or
less) evenly administered among convicted criminals. If people
think that punishments are often administered to those who are
innocent, they do not approve; if they think that minor peca-
dillos (such as smoking marijuana) are being punished with
heavy jail sentences while robbers get off scot-free, they do not
approve; if they think that whites and rich people receive
lenience while poor blacks receive harsh punishments, they do
not approve. These examples illustrate the requirements of most
people's sense of justice. People believe that punishment is one
means by which serious crime might be reduced, but they may
believe many things about fairness that reduce their punitive
reactions. We will use these facts to locate variables that might
affect approval or disapproval of punishment for crime.

To begin with, people differ in their definitions of crime:
What one person defines as an acceptable deviation another defines as a criminal offense. These variations in beliefs about the
offensiveness of certain actions could stem from two sources:
First, the law reflects particular moral standards, and people
may or may not feel that it adequately reflects their own
standards. Second, some people may be more willing than
others to tolerate deviations from their own standards. The
first is a question about the normative mean; the second is a
question about the tolerable variance. It is possible, then,
that variations in beliefs about what sorts of actions ought to
be illegal can explain variations in approval of punitiveness. We
would imagine that people who feel that the law corresponds
fairly closely to their own standards might be more punitive
than those who feel that there is little relationship between

their own morals and the law. We would further imagine that people who believe everyone should have the same morality, and that deviations from this morality ought to be corrected, would be more punitive than people with more flexible notions about morality. Such variations in definitions of morality and in tolerance are particularly important in a pluralist society, where we would expect to find variations in definitions of morality among various racial and ethnic groups, generations, classes, and religious and political groups.

In the late 1960s and early 1970s—when a good deal of the "crime" that was being punished by the justice system consisted of such offenses as participation in civil rights protests, opposition to American participation in the Vietnam War, and publication of pictures of naked people—many people doubted the appropriateness of the sentences. In these cases, punitiveness could easily be viewed as a conservative tactic to prevent social change. The need for punishment was reduced for people not considering many of these "offenses" to be offensive (see Kadish, 1967). We would thus expect people to be less punitive if they believed either that civil rights protests, opposition to the war, draft resistance, and nudity were unobjectionable or that such deviations should at any rate be tolerated; we would expect people to be more punitive if they believed that these particular deviations from the norm were serious and that all serious deviations should be punished as crimes.

People also differ in the procedures they think essential to establish guilt. Even if the act is indisputably offensive—as are the violent crimes that have been the focus of recent concern—there may still be disagreement about how likely it is that an average convicted person is actually guilty. This is due in part to different conceptions of how trustworthy police and district attorneys are and in part to different views of the frequency and relevance of mitigating circumstances.

Some people content that the probability of a defendant being arrested, charged, and found guilty varies systematically with such factors as age, education, income, race, and so forth. That is, regardless of the circumstances, an unemployed Puerto Rican is more likely than a middle-class white minister to be found guilty of robbing a liquor store. Other people believe that our criminal justice system is more unbiased than this and that differences in resources (which might enable one to hire good lawyers, find convincing witnesses, or even speak effectively in one's own defense) and personal characteristics (such as how closely one conforms to the stereotypic image of the law-abiding citizen) have little effect on the outcome of a criminal proceeding. The fact that most criminal convictions are not the result of criminal proceedings at all, but rather results of plea bargaining (Rosett, 1967), may strengthen the suspicion of bias.

A second issue concerns the moral responsibility of the "criminal" for his or her actions. Some people argue that, because of mitigating circumstances, a person who has committed an offense might still not be guilty of crime. For example, the same offender may be a burglar to one person but a confused sixteen-year-old in trouble because of an alcoholic father to another. These different conceptions of the fairness of the justice system and of degrees of guilt for the same offense may also affect punitiveness. We suspect that people who believe that the criminal justice system is biased are likely to be less punitive than those who believe it is fair. Similarly, people who have a complex and merciful view of criminal responsibility are likely to be less punitive than those who believe that all offenders are criminals.

Closely related to definitions of both crime and guilt is the requirement that punishment be more or less evenly administered. In its simple form, this means that people who are convicted of similar crimes must be punished similarly. Race, sex, age, income, and so forth should not lead to heavier (or lighter) sentences for the same offenses. More complicated versions of this requirement of equal sentencing involve recognition of the possibility of systematic variations (1) in the definitions of crimes and their corresponding punishments, (2) in the likelihood of being found guilty once charged, and (3) in the prevalence of mitigating circumstances. These systematic variations may mean that the poor are punished more than middle-class whites because their offenses are more likely to be defined as crimes and to be punished more heavily, because poor people are more likely to be convicted if charged, and because poor people may be more likely to experience the frustrations of unemployment, which might in turn lead them to commit crimes. People who believe either that punishments are not handed out equally or that other inequities in the justice system result in some groups receiving more punishments than others are likely to be less eager to punish offenders for crimes than are people who believe that the sentences are assigned fairly and that other problems in the justice system do not render it grossly unfair.

Even if everyone agrees, in a particular case, that a serious crime has been committed, that the accused is actually guilty, and that this person really ought to be punished, there might still be lack of unanimity about punishment. Punishment serves many purposes, and people disagree about how well a specific proposed punishment fulfills these functions. Theoretically, any given punishment simultaneously serves at least five purposes:

1. Punishment clarifies the norms of the community, because the process of arriving at a sentence for a crime involves negotiation about the law and current sentiment. In this sense, a sentence for a crime represents an update of the collective sentiment about that crime; recent sentences are revisions of the public's original statement (codified in law) about that moral issue.
2. Punishments are also attempts to deter criminals from committing crimes by showing them how the justice system will respond to such offenses.
3. Punishments often attempt to rehabilitate offenders both by demonstrating the seriousness of society's intention to make crime unprofitable and by inculcating a more positive orientation to society.
4. Punishment at least temporarily prevents the criminal—either through incarceration or through constant monitoring of his or her activity—from committing further crimes.
5. Finally, punishment is retribution or vengeance. It is society's way of "getting even" by inflicting pain on

those people who have unjustly harmed others. (See Zimring and Hawkins, 1973, for a similar list; see also Durkheim, 1964.)

Most debates about the functions of punishment probably concern the questions of the prevention or deterrence of crime and of the rehabilitation of criminals. Zimring and Hawkins (1973, p. 1) note that "belief in the deterrent efficacy of penal sanctions is as old as the criminal law itself." Generations of criminologists, lawyers, judges, and philosophers have concerned themselves with the morality of punishment, assuming that its deterrent, preventive, and rehabilitative effects were obvious. Only since World War II has there been much research on the effects of punishment. Zimring and Hawkins summarize the findings of many of these studies in their attempt to classify factors that condition the differential effectiveness of various legal threats. They argue that we must think in terms of marginal deterrence; we must ask whether a stiffer penalty deters, prevents, or rehabilitates better than a lighter sentence. Such issues must be considered in terms of whether the benefits of any particular policy outweigh its costs. Past research designs have not been nearly sophisticated enough to enable us to answer these questions. Very few studies can determine whether punishment has any effect at all, much less whether any given punishment is superior to any other punishment. Further, we have not been able to distinguish empirically between deterrent, preventive, and rehabilitative effects of punishment, much less specify which types of punishment fulfill which functions most efficiently. Disagreement about capital punishment is often focused on this question of marginal deterrence. Many opponents of capital punishment might favor it if they thought execution was more effective than life imprisonment in deterring homicides. The effect of capital punishment on the murder rate is sufficiently small, though, that one has to go to considerable statistical trouble to find any evidence of the deterrent effect at all, and even then the argument is not very convincing (Zimring and Hawkins, 1973).

Finally, of course, people can disagree about the morality of punishing people for public purposes, even if they agree with the public purposes and think that punishment is an effective way to achieve them. In order to have a deterrent effect or to define or clarify the norms about a particular crime success- fully, a punishment must often be more severe than the par- ticular violation itself might require. That is, society often makes an example of offenders by punishing them more severely than would be required to "teach them a lesson." Usually the additional punishment is intended to teach others the lesson as well (Zimring and Hawkins, 1973). Questions about the morality of punishing people for public purposes are particularly troublesome when the punishment involved is execution. American culture is very ambivalent about the morality of violence directed to public purposes. We celebrate such violence on television (in westerns and in police and detective shows) yet we reject it in most public policy. Men and women also seem to be socialized quite differently about the legitimacy of violence as a response to wrongdoings.

From all of the preceding points, it is clear that attitudes toward punishment of criminals are quite complex, because they are meshed with other ideas about moral standards and toler- ance of differences in values, about what it means to be guilty of a crime and how guilt can be proven, about the functions of punishment and the effectiveness of particular punishments, and so forth. When a respondent gives a lenient answer to a question about the harshness of local courts or appropriate- ness of capital punishment, we do not know whether this is because the respondent thinks (1) the courts often convict innocent people, (2) the justice system assigns sentences that will have no beneficial effect, or some other reason. Some of this confusion about the exact interpretation of public opinion measures could be eliminated by asking more detailed questions about a respondent's systematic beliefs concerning punishment, deterrence, retributive sanctions, and so on.

Liberalism and Attitudes Toward Punishment

We saw in Chapter Three that people who are afraid of crime in their own neighborhoods or who think crime is the nation's most important problem are more punitive than other people because they are more concerned with preventing crime. We also found, though, that fear of crime and thinking that crime is an important problem are rather unsteady predictors of punitive attitudes. One possible reason for the weakness of these relationships is that punitive attitudes are part of a general liberal world view.

When we discuss the liberal world view, we are talking about a belief system. Converse (1964, p. 207) defines a belief system as "a configuration of ideas and attitudes in which the elements are bound together by some form of constraint or functional interdependence." By "constraint," Converse is referring to our ability to predict other attitudes once we have information about an initial specific attitude. The level of constraint is generally measured by the correlations between various attitudes. Converse argues that the sources of constraint in systems of beliefs are not logical consistency but psychological consistency—whether or not respondents hold a group of ideas as an interpretable cluster—and social consistency—a constraint on interest and information, especially information of the contextual sort. In short, if we want to study a world view, we must look for ideas that are associated with each other historically. Having found such a group of ideas, we must look for a set of circumstances in the present that makes this association important or salient to the respondents or that gives the respondents access to particular information. Finally, we must check to see whether these ideas or attitudes correlate. (The literature in political science related to these issues includes Achen, 1975; Converse, 1970; Field and Anderson, 1969; Margolis, 1977; Nie, Verba, and Petrocik, 1976; and Pierce and Rose, 1974.)

By general liberalism we refer to a division of popular opinion that started during the Enlightenment and concerned civil liberty, equality under the law, labor law, and prison reform. These concerns have been or become part of American liberalism, with which they have been associated for at least two centuries.

American liberalism has been the concern of Williams

51), McCloskey (1963), Heberle (1951), and Myrdal (1962), ng others. In discussing the ideology of liberal democracy, Williams argues that its most distinguishing characteristic is a commitment to toleration—both "essential toleration" of groups who are potential alternative governments and "nonessential toleration" of minorities and unpopular ideas. He claims that the ideology of liberal democracy is a tacit, barebones ideology—the "*smallest* ideology that can actually survive" (1961, pp. 379, 384). McCloskey agrees with Williams on both counts, contending that American political thought, institutions, and behavior all exhibit a fundamental ambivalence. This ambivalence, or tolerance of mutually inconsistent beliefs, together with a pragmatic spirit, are the basic traits of the American ideology. Heberle, discussing liberalism as a social movement, notes that although it has been in existence since the Enlightenment, both the ideas and groups associated with it have changed over the years. While the economic goal of laissez-faire and the bourgeois liberals who championed it have been fairly transient, the goals of liberty and equality seem to have been more persistent.

Finally, Myrdal discusses the "American creed" and its dispersion throughout American society, claiming that compared with other Western nations, America has "the *most explicitly expressed* system of general ideas in reference to human interrelations" and that this body of ideals is both widely understood and widely appreciated (1962, p. 3). Essentially, the American creed is a humanistic liberalism developed during the Enlightenment, when the United States attained both its national consciousness and its political structure. The two basic values are liberty and equality, with equality taking precedence (as Tocqueville, 1945, noted years earlier). Myrdal's discussion of the American tradition of inscribing ideals in laws is particularly relevant, because the American tendency to codify ideals means that in the United States, more than in other nations, there tends to be more national debate over such ideals as equality before the law, freedom of speech, racial integration, etc.

All four authors agree that equality, liberty, and particularly tolerance are central to American liberalism. This is important because it means that there are some basic ideas, however vague, which are commonly acknowledged to "belong together" and collectively are given legitimacy as the essence of liberal Americanism. When such a set of ideas exists and has wide legitimacy, it can act as a magnet to attract and bind related ideas. Further, when such a group of ideas is embodied in national institutions and structures, people who might not normally be concerned with these ideas must confront them, because national-level disputes about them will affect a large portion of the populace. Finally, as each of the authors agrees, the important question is whether these values or attitudes are related *psychologically*—strict logical consistency really has little to do with it. A historical tradition and legal codification are very likely to encourage a psychological association between the ideas in question.

In recent history, we can document the continuing importance of this liberal world view by examining survey data on attitudes toward civil liberties, abortion, sexual liberalism, and feminism. Each of these issues is related to the liberal tradition and concerns a freedom or right enshrined in our constitution; each has, therefore, been the focus of numerous legal battles. We know that attitudes on each of these issues have been becoming more liberal in recent years (Davis, 1975; Taylor, 1977; Smith, 1976b), and we can document this trend by looking at correlations between scales composed of items related to these four issues. In the 1974 General Social Survey, there were twelve questions on civil liberties attitudes. These questions asked whether atheists, communists, socialists, or homosexuals should be allowed to give public speeches, teach in colleges, and have books they had written placed in public libraries (see Appendix for question wordings). Combining these twelve questions into an additive scale provides us with a measure of "Enlightenment liberalism" that correlates with a scale of five questions measuring liberal sexual attitudes at .587, with a scale of six opinions on legalized abortion at .253, and with a scale of four feminism questions at .457. That is, the Enlightenment tradition is still relevant, and a respondent's civil liberties score should be a fairly good measure of adherence to that tradition.

We must now show why punitive attitudes should be re-

lated to the Enlightenment tradition. This argument has two
parts: First, attitudes toward punishment were historically part
of the Enlightenment tradition. Broadly speaking, the humani-
tarian aspects of the Enlightenment were closely related to
prison reform and to the abolition of capital punishment, while
the civil aspects of the Enlightenment involved fair courts, laws
protecting the poor, and limitation of the power of all public
authorities. Insofar as these currents of public opinion have
historic continuity, we would expect that those people who are
more liberal on questions like civil liberty would also be more
liberal (or more lenient) on questions of punitiveness. If one
wants to limit authorities in the interests of civil liberty, one
might want to limit authorities in the ways they deal with
criminals. If, in contrast, one believes that the central problem
of modern society is the decay of authority—reflected in the
rising crime rate and the proliferation of pornography, atheism,
and disrespect for one's elders—then one might endorse both
the restriction of civil liberties and also harsher treatment of
criminals.

Second, both punitive attitudes and liberal (or conservative) world views are related to the components of fair punishment. We argued earlier that people could disapprove of punishment for many reasons: They believe that some offenses currently defined as crimes should not be illegal, that some people
convicted of crimes are not actually guilty, that mitigating circumstances make questions of legal guilt irrelevant, that punishment is often administered more harshly to some categories of
offenders than to others, that punishment does not fulfill the
functions it is supposed to, that the benefits of a particular
punishment do not make up for its costs, or that a given punishment is simply inherently immoral. Liberals and conservatives
typically take opposite positions on these individual issues. For
example, liberals have traditionally believed that the law should
permit greater variations in morality, while conservatives have
tended to favor stricter limits on personal freedom. Thus we
would expect that more liberals than conservatives would
oppose punishment because they believe that the offense in
question should not be considered a crime. Similarly, liberals
are probably more likely to believe that we should reduce sen-

tences when there are mitigating circumstances; that the criminal justice system administers punishments unevenly; that the courts and police may accuse, try, convict, and punish innocent people; that no public purpose merits punishment by execution; and so forth. Because liberals are more likely to think that punishment is often unfair, they have more reasons to oppose it. In general, then, we would expect that liberals would be more likely to give lenient responses.

Are Liberals More Lenient?

In the preceding section we established correlations between a civil liberties scale and other scales whose substance should be related to the American liberal tradition. We concluded that a respondent's score on the civil liberties scale should be a fairly good measure of his or her adherence to the Enlightenment tradition. In this section we will discuss the relation between liberalism (as measured by the civil liberties score) and attitudes toward the punishment of criminals.

Combining five years of data, the correlation between a six-item civil liberties scale and an additive scale composed of the two punitive attitude items was .166 for whites alone and .142 with blacks included. That is, if there is a general tendency to be punitive—measured by the capital punishment and harsher courts questions—and if there is an Enlightenment tradition measured by the civil liberties questions, then the Enlightenment tradition is slightly related to punitiveness in public opinion. But if civil liberties measures the Enlightenment tradition, then liberalism on women's issues, abortion, race, and sex questions are much closer to the core of that tradition than is punitiveness, and this is shown by their higher correlations with civil libertarianism.

When we examine this relationship in more detail, even the slight relationship of punitiveness and liberalism seems to be mostly due to a very few extreme liberals. Table 25 breaks down both scales into extreme groups in order to pinpoint the source of the association that accounts for the .166 correlation in the white population. The respondents are broken down into those who answered both punitiveness questions so as to

Table 25. Punitiveness Toward Criminals and Civil Liberties Scores
(Whites Only)

(a) Percentages (and raw frequencies) of respondents			
	Civil liberties scores		
Punitiveness	All liberal	Intermediate	Half or more conservative
Lenient on both questions	5.7 (74)	1.9 (28)	.9 (25)
Intermediate	48.0 (619)	38.4 (562)	33.5 (951)
Punitive on both questions	46.2 (596)	59.7 (874)	65.7 (1866)
Total	99.9 (1289)	100.0 (1464)	100.1 (2842)

(b) Odds ratios for subtables		
	Civil liberties scores	
Punitiveness	All liberal versus intermediate	Intermediate versus conservative
Lenient versus intermediate	2.399	1.895
Intermediate versus punitive	1.615	1.262

Source: General Social Surveys, 1972-1974 and 1976-1977. Data including blacks show a slightly greater concentration in the "All Liberal/Lenient on both" cell.

indicate they were inclined to be lenient with criminals (they said their local courts were "too harsh" and they opposed capital punishment for murder); those who gave mixed, intermediate, or "don't know" answers; and those who answered both questions punitively (they thought local courts were "not harsh enough" and they favored capital punishment for murder). Likewise, the civil liberties scores are broken down into three categories: the "all liberal" response pattern, which includes those answering all twelve questions in a liberal direction; the "intermediate" group, which includes those answering more than half (but not all twelve) of the questions liberally; and the "conservative" scorers, who answer at least half of the questions conservatively.

The top panel of the table gives the percentage distribution of whites' answers on punitiveness by opinion on civil liberties. The most striking pattern in the table is that much of the association is in the first row, and most of that first-row association involves the upper left cell. That is, there is a marked overrepresentation of people who answered all twelve of the civil liberties questions in a liberal direction and who are also inclined to treat criminals leniently.

The second panel of Table 25 restates this information by giving the odds ratios for the different parts of the tabulation. That is, the odds ratio of 2.399 in the "liberal versus intermediate" column and the "lenient versus intermediate" row means that the odds of being lenient on criminals if one is all-liberal on questions of civil liberty are 2.399 times as great as the odds of being lenient on criminals if one is intermediate on questions of civil liberty. More briefly, Enlightenment liberals are 2.399 times as likely as intermediates to give lenient responses (as opposed to intermediate ones) to questions about social control. Likewise, we find that liberals are 1.615 times as likely as intermediates to give intermediate as opposed to punitive answers. The association between Enlightenment liberalism and social control attitudes due to the overrepresentation of the "lenients" among those who are all-liberal on civil liberties is greater than it is anywhere else in the table.

Another way to look at this is to ask how many lenient all-liberals we would have to subtract from the upper left cell in order to make the association in the upper left subtable the same as the association in the other subtables. If we subtract twenty-five "bleeding heart liberals" from the upper left cell, then the odds ratio in the upper left subtable would be 1.589 which is very near 1.591, which is the average odds ratio of the other three subtables. Thus a great deal of the association between civil libertarianism and being lenient on criminals is due to a small number of people (about .4 percent of the population) who take extreme positions on both sets of issues.

The same general result holds for the other scales measuring the Enlightenment tradition: about twenty people who give all-liberal answers on these other scales and who give lenient answers on social control questions account for much of the association between liberalism and lenience, and removing these respondents produces a more regular table.

In summary, there may be a very small part of the total

population, roughly 1 percent, whose members tend to answer all liberalism questions in a liberal direction *and* who also answer liberally those questions that have to do with punishments for crimes. The rest of the population sees a weaker connection between these questions of Enlightenment liberalism (civil liberties, sexual liberalism, feminism, and abortion liberalism) and the treatment of criminals by the courts.

Is the Effect of Liberalism on Punitiveness Stable?

The effect of liberalism on punitiveness appears to be small, based on our data from the General Social Surveys. However, in Chapter Three we found that the relationship between fear and wanting harsher courts was reasonably strong during the 1960s but had virtually disappeared by the 1970s. We want to know, then, whether the weakness of the relation between liberalism and punitiveness is also a recent phenomenon. Perhaps the high salience of the crime problem in the 1970s has had such an impact on the population that nothing as ephemeral as liberalism (or at least, no liberalism short of the extreme variety) could temper the punitive response.

The most commonly asked questions measuring the Enlightenment tradition in the United States concern race relations, and the most commonly asked question on punitiveness is about support for capital punishment. As an operational matter, then, the only light we can shed on the question of the stability of liberalism's impact on lenience toward criminals comes from the relationship between race relations questions and capital punishment attitudes. We have not used race relations questions as measures of liberalism earlier, because racial issues involve a large regional difference above and beyond any regional variation in liberalism itself. The use of race relations questions as an indicator of the respondent's general liberal or conservative outlook thus adds considerable "noise" to our analysis. However, we have no other measures of liberalism that appear on the same surveys with questions about punishment of criminals, so we have no choice but to use the race relations questions if we wish to learn anything about the relation between liberalism and punitiveness. Because "race relations" means quite different things in the North than in the South, and because capital punishment also evidently means quite different things to men and women, we control for sex and region in the analysis that follows.

Our first measure of racial liberalism is a question about laws against marriage between blacks and whites. This question was asked in 1964 and again in the 1972-1975 General Social Surveys. Table 26 shows that people who favor laws against intermarriage also tend to favor capital punishment. On the average (weighted), there was a difference of 1.8 percent between those who favored laws against intermarriage and those who opposed such laws in 1964, and about a 7.6 percent difference in the 1970s. When we control for racial attitudes, Southerners seem to be slightly less in favor of capital punishment than Northerners, and this gap is especially evident among prejudiced women. The most important result, however, is that there is no general tendency for the relation between punitiveness and liberalism (as measured by this race relations item) to decline as the crime problem became more salient in the 1970s. If anything, the relation between liberalism and lenience increased.

A second measure of racial liberalism is provided by the question on attitudes toward school integration asked in 1964, 1972, and in 1976-1977. Table 27 examines the relationship between attitudes toward school integration and attitudes toward capital punishment. This relationship is weaker than the relationship between attitudes toward intermarriage and positions on capital punishment, but on the average there is a 5.8 percent difference (weighted) between those who favor school integration and those who oppose it, with opponents of school integration being more punitive. Further, there is no evidence here that the relationship between liberalism and punitive attitudes is decreasing.

Overall, then, it seems that there has been a slight relationship between a general liberal current of opinion and lenience toward criminals but that much of this relationship is due to a very few ideological liberals who view penal philos-

Table 26. Attitudes Toward Capital Punishment and Interracial Marriage by Region of Residence and Sex of the Respondent (Whites Only)

Percentages favoring capital punishment

Laws against intermarriage	Sex and Region			
	Northern males	Southern males	Northern females	Southern females
1964:				
Oppose law (favor intermarriage)	67.5 (286)[a]	59.6 (57)	47.9 (236)	41.2 (34)
Favor law	63.2 (261)	67.5 (154)	54.6 (339)	42.1 (190)
1972-1978:				
Oppose Law	71.5 (1804)	72.1 (538)	61.5 (1937)	63.5 (531)
Favor Law	82.4 (722)	78.9 (521)	70.9 (844)	59.2 (625)

Source: 1964 NORC survey (SRS 760) and the 1972-1978 General Social Surveys combined. The wording of the capital punishment question is quite different in the 1964 survey than in the other surveys; see Appendix for exact question wordings.

[a]Raw frequencies indicated in parentheses.

Table 27. Attitudes Toward Capital Punishment and School Integration by Region of Residence and Sex of Respondent (Whites Only)

Percentages favoring capital punishment

Blacks and whites should attend:	Sex and Region			
	Northern males	Southern males	Northern females	Southern females
1964:				
Same schools	64.3 (420)[a]	61.0 (59)	49.3 (418)	35.0 (60)
Different schools	66.4 (134)	67.8 (149)	57.1 (163)	43.8 (162)
1972:				
Same schools	69.0 (436)	68.9 (119)	58.5 (415)	42.5 (87)
Different schools	78.0 (41)	66.7 (36)	68.8 (32)	37.3 (59)
1976-1977:				
Same schools	78.7 (728)	77.2 (259)	66.5 (875)	68.5 (267)
Different schools	86.6 (67)	81.9 (94)	81.6 (76)	64.7 (119)

Source: 1964 NORC survey (SRS 760), 1972 General Social Survey, and 1976-1977 General Social Surveys combined.

[a]Raw frequencies indicated in parentheses.

ophy as a part of their liberalism. Punitiveness is not a major part of a more encompassing view of the appropriate relative roles of authorities and citizens. However, what little relationship there is remains stable over time.

Busing and Punitive Attitudes

We have found that the general liberal world view, as measured either by the civil liberties scale or the race relations questions, does not have much to do with punitiveness or lenience except among ideological liberals. One race relations item does have a very strong relationship to punitiveness, though—the question asking the respondent's attitude toward busing. Other analyses indicate that support for busing does not function as other race relations items do, that it is not very highly correlated with those items, and that it has different causes and effects (Kelley, 1974; Erbe, 1977). Busing is thus a different sort of race relations item, and this difference is closely related to the difference between punitive attitudes and other attitudes that form the core of Enlightenment liberalism. Kelley, for example, finds that racism is related to political intolerance, women's issues, attitudes toward sexual permissiveness, and abortion, while attitudes toward busing are related to punitiveness. That is, most race relations items are part of the "general liberalism complex," but busing does not seem to be a deep and integral part of that complex. In this chapter we have found that attitudes toward punishment are not part of that complex either. It is thus no surprise that punitiveness and opposition to busing are highly correlated. Explaining this correlation is, of course, quite another matter.

Briefly, busing and crime have several elements in common: both involve (1) a racial element, (2) contact with the courts, (3) physical intrusion into communities, (4) contact with the ghetto, and (5) a conflict about basic values and how they should be achieved. While all race relations items involve points (1) and (5), busing is more strongly connected with the other three points. Perhaps these other elements, shared with crime, make busing a social control issue. In this section we will argue that two of these elements—contact with the ghetto and contact with the courts—are especially critical.

Regarding contact with the ghetto, we demonstrated in previous chapters that black males are overrepresented among people arrested for serious crimes, that crime rates are higher in the integrated and predominantly black areas of large cities, and also that fear is similarly concentrated in these ghetto areas. Thus, questions about fear and about punishment of crime are in some sense questions about how to manage the social control problems of integrated and all-black urban neighborhoods. Similarly, the problem of overcrowded, segregated schools is also a dilemma of the ghetto, and questions about busing are therefore also questions about what should be done about the ghetto. Given this interpretation and the fact that neither the busing question nor the social control questions correlate very highly with other race relations questions, we believe that attitudes toward busing and punitiveness are fundamentally different from other questions about race relations. While the other race questions ask about contact with individual blacks, questions about busing and punitiveness have little to do with race except insofar as the inhabitants of the ghetto tend to be predominantly black. That is, the busing question involves considering what will happen when a large group of ghetto children are moved into a neighborhood school in a white community. This is quite a different question in people's minds than the question of whether a neighbor's child who happens to be black should attend the mostly white neighborhood school. Similarly, questions about punishment of criminals are really about whether greater punitiveness will reduce crime in the currently unmanageable streets of the ghetto. This is not the same question as whether one's neighbor, who might also be black, should be imprisoned.

Questions about busing and questions about punishment also both concern the authority of the courts. Busing has not been adopted by a legislative body in any large city to solve its ethnic and/or educational problems (except in certain deviant cases such as Berkeley, California). Instead, it is a court-ordered solution to a situation—namely, discriminatory government by local school boards—which not everyone agrees is a problem. The point is that although there are many nonconstitutional arguments in favor of busing to achieve school integration, these arguments have only very rarely convinced a political body in the United States. The constitutional argument, in contrast, has frequently persuaded the courts. Questions about busing are thus intimately related to larger questions about the role of the courts in helping govern society. One thing that the busing question might measure, then, is an attitude that "the courts probably have good reasons for what they are doing and, though I may be unhappy with this particular decision, I am willing to recognize that the courts and their ways of reasoning are important elements in the health of the social system." Likewise, the question on whether courts should be harsher explicitly asks whether the courts, as they stand, can be trusted. Further, the abolition of capital punishment was, by and large, carried out in the United States by the courts on constitutional principles rather than by the legislatures on principles of political wisdom and social health. In short, we can reasonably argue that each of these three issues—busing, harshness of courts, and capital punishment—is at least partly concerned with the respondent's view of the role of the courts and his or her willingness to allow the courts to decide how to solve major social problems.

Stinchcombe and Taylor (1980) have studied the relationship between respect for courts and busing attitudes in more detail in a study of the Boston school desegregation controversy. While the sample did not include enough people who supported busing to make the analysis of that question very worthwhile, it was profitable to study the degree of opposition to busing as it related to attitude toward the court. Using measures of the degree of opposition to busing both as expressed in words and as manifest in action, they found that the crucial attitude was a willingness to grant the court the right to make decisions *against the will of the majority of the people.*

A populist ideology holds that the job of the courts is to execute the will of the people in particular cases. It is quite clear that the people oppose busing to integrate schools and favor punishment of robbers, murderers, rapists, and assailants; thus, the job of the courts, in the populist view, is to oppose busing and to punish criminals. A constitutionalist ideology, in contrast, argues that the courts have a duty to defend higher principles—principles of just administration of school systems and principles of due process of law for the accused—regardless of the current state of popular opinion. In Boston we found that constitutionalists supported the court and populists were in opposition.

A series of questions measuring reactions to court-ordered desegregation by busing asked specifically whether the courts had duties to eliminate unlawful segregation, whether courts have the right to make decisions that many people disagree with, whether the judge who ordered busing in Boston had the right to do so, whether federal judges were competent to draw up desegregation plans, and whether school officials can legitimately delay their constitutional duty to obey the court. Pro-judiciary responses to all these questions acknowledge the higher duty of the court to go against public opinion when constitutional principles require it.

If we study only people who disagree with the court on the specific question of busing, we find a very strong relationship between support for such actions as boycotts of the schools and contempt for the courts' constitutional role. Those who believe that courts must sometimes go against public opinion are less likely to join a boycott, even if they agree with the purpose of the boycott. What this shows for our argument is that attitudes toward busing are very closely related to attitudes about the constitutional role of the court to oppose public opinion. Hence it is not hard to imagine that people who support the courts' constitutional role would think that there is probably good reason for a local court to give out the punishments it does rather than harsher punishments and that there might be reason and justice in the constitutional arguments against capital punishment. If judges should resist popular clamor against busing when it is their constitutional duty, then they should resist popular clamor for draconian punishments when it is their constitutional duty. This particular kind of liberalism, then, supports judicial elitism based on specialized understanding of and responsibility for constitu-

tional principles. The small minority of the population who
support the busing and support the lenience now meted out by
the courts may connect the two issues together by supporting
this judicial elitism.

Thus far, we have argued that busing and punitiveness
are both questions about how to manage the problems of the
ghetto and, further, that they are questions about the legitimacy of court-imposed solutions to these problems. To over-
state the matter rhetorically, it could be that they ask: "Can
the problems of the ghetto be solved by the courts using traditional constitutional principles?"

Though this argument may capture the essence of what
busing and punitiveness questions have in common, it certainly
does not sound very plausible on a psychological level. Perhaps we can construct a more likely picture that still involves
the principle enunciated above. Many whites, and at least some
blacks, consider the ghetto itself to be a powerful cause of evil
effects. To some degree, racial prejudice against individual black
people may thus be caused more by the belief that they carry
the ghetto with them than by any bad feelings toward people
of another race. Similarly, prejudice against the ghetto may
often be due not to its being inhabited by black people but to
the fact that the ghetto is an unpleasant place in which to live
or even to live near. High violent crime rates, garbage in the
streets, low reading test scores, and broken families all may
be seen as a collective phenomenon—the ghetto—against which
one wants to be protected. The question our respondents are
being asked is whether ordinary school administration (in the
busing question) and ordinary law enforcement (in the courts
question) are enough to contain this collective source of evil
effects.

Superficially the answer to this question is obvious. The
average sentence per serious crime known to the police is about
one month in prison. These sentences do not seem to have
cured the crime epidemic in the ghetto. Further, the same
school systems that run the predominantly white schools in
the big city also run the ghetto schools, though they do not
seem to be doing such a good job with the latter. If the present

educational and criminal justice systems have been unable to solve the social problems of the ghetto, one might wonder why they should be expected to perform any better in the future. People who believe that our current educational and criminal justice systems can contain the evil effects of the ghetto may believe that we can solve the problem of the ghetto if we simply extend to black children the services that have always been available to white children in their neighborhood schools and if we extend firm but fair treatment in the courts to black criminals.

We have argued that attitudes toward punishment of criminals and toward busing might be related because both concern whether ghetto problems can be solved by the courts using traditional constitutional principles. We also attempted to show that this connection between the two issues was plausible on a psychological level. Now we must turn to the data to see if the connection between punitiveness and attitudes toward busing has remained constant over the years for which we have data.

Tables 28 and 29 outline the changes in the relationship between busing attitudes and punitiveness over the time period for which we have data. Because busing attitudes are related to region and capital punishment attitudes are related to sex, we present the data separately by region and sex.

We find, first, that in both tables in all the categories for which we have sufficient data, the level of punitiveness increased between 1972 and 1974-1975 and again between 1974-1975 and 1976-1978. Second, as the South became more similar to the North in busing attitudes, there was also a convergence in levels of punitiveness. Third, we have found in other analyses in this and in Chapter Three that many relationships between punitiveness and other variables disappeared over time as the public became more uniformly punitive in the 1970s. A similar trend appears in both Tables 28 and 29. The relationship between busing attitudes and punitiveness was quite strong in 1972 but had become weaker by 1974-1975 and still weaker by 1976-1978.

The relationship between punitive attitudes and busing

Table 28. Assessments of Harshness of Local Courts, Attitudes Toward Busing, Region of Residence, and Sex of Respondent[a]

(Whites Only)

Percentage who think the courts are "not harsh enough"

	Region and Sex			
Busing attitudes	Northern males	Southern males	Northern females	Southern females
1972:				
For	50.7 (75)[c]	b (11)	41.8 (79)	b (9)
Against	76.5 (412)	71.5 (151)	75.3 (392)	62.7 (158)
1974-1975:				
For	70.5 (78)	69.2 (39)	66.7 (117)	70.5 (44)
Against	83.4 (512)	84.2 (241)	82.3 (565)	83.1 (284)
1976-1978:				
For	76.7 (163)	78.3 (60)	71.7 (279)	75.0 (52)
Against	86.8 (1043)	84.3 (464)	85.9 (1231)	83.9 (622)

Source: General Social Surveys, 1972, 1974-1975 combined, and 1976-1978 combined.

[a]Respondents answering variant wording of the courts question in 1974 were excluded. "Don't Know" and "About Right" as well as "Too Harsh" were included as non-punitive answers.

[b]Too few cases for reliable percentages.

[c]Raw frequencies indicated in parentheses.

Table 29. Attitudes Toward Capital Punishment and Busing by Region of Residence and Sex of Respondent (Whites Only)

Percentage favoring capital punishment

	Region and Sex			
Busing attitudes	Northern males	Southern females	Northern males	Southern females
1972:				
For	45.7 (70)	a (10)	45.1 (71)	a (9)
Against	74.9 (399)	70.6 (143)	62.6 (358)	43.0 (135)
1974-1975:				
For	51.9 (104)	55.1 (49)	51.3 (154)	51.0 (49)
Against	77.0 (673)	78.5 (307)	68.6 (700)	66.6 (347)
1976-1978:				
For	65.0 (157)	69.6 (56)	55.6 (261)	70.0 (50)
Against	81.3 (1018)	80.2 (450)	71.1 (1161)	69.1 (564)

Source: General Social Surveys, 1972, 1974-1975 combined, and 1976-1978 combined.

[a]Too few cases for reliable percentages.

[b]Raw frequencies indicated in parentheses.

attitudes is stronger than the relationships we found between other individual-level variables and punitive attitudes. It is more nearly comparable in size to the relationship we found between punitiveness and extreme liberalism (answering all twelve civil liberties questions in a liberal direction). This in turn suggests that the process of attitude formation is qualitatively different at the liberal extreme than over the rest of the spectrum of public opinion. If we distinguish the extreme liberals (probusing, against harsher sentencing in the courts, against capital punishment, and "all liberal" on a number of scales of social and political liberalism) from those who are moderately liberal, many social variables cease to play a causal role. That is, most social variables that are related to moderate liberalism fail to explain extreme liberalism. Instead, only other measures of extreme liberalism play any important role in predicting any one of these measures of extreme liberalism. This is important to our analysis of social control attitudes, because as the rest of the population becomes more punitive, Enlightenment liberals continue to represent the bastion of lenience.

Summary

In Chapter Three we set out to study the causes of fear of crime and the relationship between salience of crime (as measured by fear and by ratings of the nation's most important problem) and punitiveness. We found that, for the most part, fear of crime was determined by very sensible causes. But when we examined the hypothesis that people who were afraid or who thought crime was an important problem would be more punitive, we found ourselves at sea. Though people who are afraid do tend to be more punitive, this relationship is not nearly strong enough to account for the increase in punitiveness in the last two decades.

In this chapter, therefore, we examined another piece of the puzzle. Figure 2 illustrates the various relationships we examined. Because of the historical association between liberalism and lenience, one might predict that an increase in liberalism would be associated with a decrease in punitiveness.

General liberal attitudes have been becoming more prevalent, and thus one might expect that opposition to capital punishment and harsh prison sentences would also be increasing. This has not been the case. Changes over time seem to bear out relations between variables which are the opposite of the individual-level relationships between these variables: more liberal (that is, recent) years are more punitive, but more liberal people are less punitive.

Figure 2. Interrelationship of Variables in Chapter Four

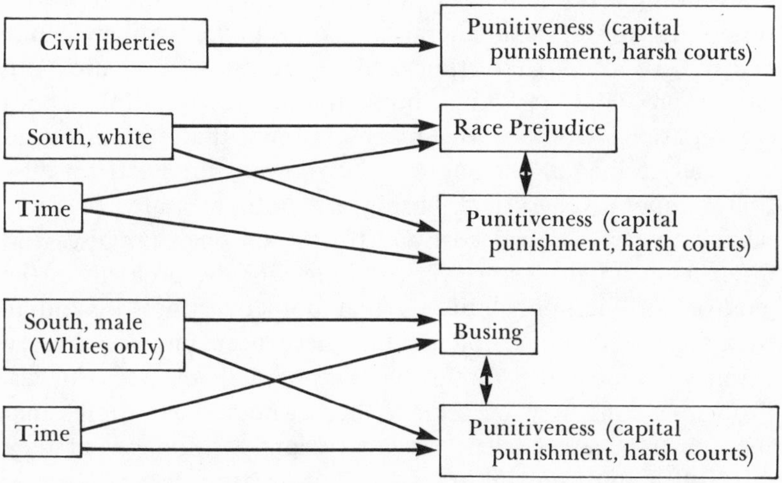

For at least some part of the population, however, lenience is part of a general world view involving other conceptions of how the social order should be organized. Liberals do tend to be more lenient with criminals, but this relationship is very modest indeed. The correlation between civil liberties attitudes and punitiveness is only about half that between civil liberties attitudes and feminism or sexual liberalism. Further, much of the relationship between liberalism and lenience is created by a very few people who answer all the liberalism questions liberally and both punitiveness questions leniently. Thus if we use the correlation between liberalism and punitiveness to predict what will happen to punitiveness, we would not expect to have much luck, because most of that prediction would have to do with the 1 percent of the population who (because of the nonlinearity of the relationship between liberalism and punitiveness) account for much of the relationship. This is fortunate for our explanatory purpose, however, because liberalism has been increasing, and this would lead us to predict decreases in punitiveness, while in fact punitiveness has been increasing.

The strongest correlation in this chapter is also one of the hardest to interpret. This is the relationship between busing attitudes and punitiveness. One interesting clue is that neither a probusing attitude nor lenience is very highly correlated with other measures of racial liberalism. This is particularly intriguing because we know that crime and segregated schools are both ghetto problems and thus implicitly involve questions about race relations. One possible interpretation is that both measures are really asking about public policy toward the ghetto itself—that nonpunitiveness and busing are both measures of being willing to pay a social cost and to restrain one's impulses and interests in order to solve (in the long run) the problem of the ghetto. Another possibility is that both questions ask public opinion about public policies that have been imposed on the country by the courts rather than by popularly elected officials. Both questions may be asking, then, whether one thinks that the courts have sufficiently good reasons for doing what they do. Still a third possibility is that busing attitudes are another measure of the extreme form of liberal consistency, which leads a respondent to answer all twelve civil liberties questions in a liberal direction or to oppose increased punishment of criminals. We can construct a convincing argument of how these three explanations might be connected in people's minds: Extreme liberals might believe that ghetto conditions can be eliminated by well-meaning teachers, by justice for blacks in trouble, and by judges who act as the official preservers of long-run constitutional values. Of course, the evidence does not speak to the validity of this seductive explanation. We will present further evidence on the circumstances under which busing and punitive attitudes are related in Chapter Six.

5

Gun Control—
Pro and Con

One possible response to violent crime is to try to control the crime by controlling the means; and one of the principal means —that makes violent crime so dangerous—is the gun. Consequently questions on gun control might tap another response to the increased salience of crime. The trend data presented in Chapter Two, however, showed that during a period when punitiveness was increasing, gun control attitudes were not changing. If gun control attitudes remain steady in the face of increased crime, increased media coverage of crime, increased salience of crime among the general public, and increased punitiveness, then it is not likely that there is any simple relationship between crime, fear of crime, and gun control attitudes.

In this chapter we show how gun ownership has interacted with fear of crime and punitiveness to stabilize attitudes toward gun control. The principal thesis of this chapter is that gun ownership (rather than gun control attitudes) is in many ways similar to a social control attitude. Consequently, the

analysis of gun ownership is a relatively straightforward ex-
tension of all that has gone before. We will show that there is a
strong relationship between punitive attitudes and gun ownership and that people who own guns are more inclined to favor
capital punishment and harsher treatment of criminals by the
courts. Gun ownership, in turn, is related to gun control attitudes in the way one might expect—gun owners do not see how
crime would be reduced by registering themselves. Fear of
crime, however, is negatively related to gun ownership. In other
words, people who own guns are less afraid to walk alone in
their neighborhoods. But this is almost entirely a spurious
relationship, because people who own guns are more likely to
live out in the country and are more likely to be male, and both
rural residents and men tend to be less afraid. Once one controls
for neighborhood and sex, there is no appreciable relation
between fear and ownership.

Figure 3 shows the causal links in this argument. On the
left are various determinants of exposure to and involvement in
the rural hunting tradition. The variables we are measuring are
on the right side of Figure 3. In hunting regions, the distance to
an area of sparse settlement in which one can hunt is likely to
be small, especially for people who live in small towns. (By
"hunting" region we generally mean all regions outside the
Northeast.) Rural residence, therefore, increases exposure to
hunting culture. It is also likely to reflect a culture originating
in the settlement of the frontier more than it reflects immigrant
society with its relatively small emphasis on hunting culture
(Kennett and Anderson, 1975).

Rural hunting cultures are strongly differentiated by sex:
people with guns are disproportionately male. Region, rural
residence, and sex therefore predict exposure to the rural
hunting culture. We established in earlier chapters that people
have been more punitive recently than they were a decade
ago. We will show shortly that there is a congruent change in
gun ownership, at least in the ownership of pistols.

The reason for the vagueness of the adjectives in the
previous paragraph (*hunting, frontier*) is that different attitude
and behavior variables are related differently to this complex

Figure 3. Interrelationship of Variables in Chapter Five

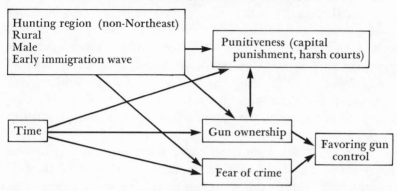

of "causes." The "hunting region" is not a well-defined entity; in literary history it would be reflected by some combination of elements from Mark Twain, William Faulkner, and Ernest Hemingway. It might be called a "macho" culture, except that contempt for women is not a major element of it. In fact, this culture tends to be historically associated with stable nuclear families in which housewives are responsible for running the house while the husbands or sons farmed, hunted, logged, prospected, or rode down the Mississippi on a raft. At the present time, as we will show, there is no relation between gun ownership and "macho" attitudes.

We find that there is a moderately strong negative relation between hunting culture and fear of crime. There are both spatial and cultural reasons for this: First, rural areas are in fact a good deal safer than urban areas, and the hunting culture is found primarily in rural areas. Second, there are elements of the hunting culture that work against fear as an appropriate response; manly courage, especially in defense of farms and women, is an important part of the culture. Hunting cultures have also been associated with the swift and certain punishment of criminals, so this combination of variables and punitiveness is positively related.

Figure Three also shows a double-headed arrow between punitiveness and gun ownership. We will find that in fact attitudes toward capital punishment or being harsh on criminals are fairly strongly related to gun ownership. The nature of that relation is presumably twofold: First, the use of guns is a traditional element of the culture which also includes vigilante justice and manly courage in self-defense. Being part of this culture probably increases the chances both of learning various practices that involve the use of guns and of believing in swift "wild West" justice. Second, being involved in hunting and shooting is likely to bring one into social circles in which there is a preference for violent summary justice, so gun ownership causes punitiveness.

A final observation on our arrangement of variables in Figure 3 is our conclusion that once the relation of frontier culture and fear of crime to residence and sex is controlled, there is virtually no effect of fear of crime on gun ownership. This finding was discussed more fully in Chapter Three.

The gun control question itself is strongly related to gun ownership and weakly related to fear of crime—both in the expected directions. Fear of crime increases endorsement of gun control, while gun ownership decreases endorsement. This causal pattern affects the stability of gun control attitudes over time; that is, a push against gun control is created as people increase their punitiveness and their gun ownership over time. But as people experience increased levels of fear, they become more inclined to want to control guns. Because this increase in fear has gone on over the same period, it tends to balance out the trend toward higher levels of gun ownership. The over-time influence on gun control attitudes is small in both cases, and the net influence is practically zero.

The Social Distribution of Gun Ownership

After finding no trends in various sets of tables tracing gun ownership over time, we have decided to combine the six available surveys to outline the social geography of gun owner-ship. Table 30 shows the relationship between gun ownership and various indicators of exposure to rural hunting culture. We have controlled for race, because it is clear that blacks did not experience the frontier culture of the South in the same way whites did. The first section of the table shows that a regional

Table 30. Gun Ownership by Region, Religion, and City Size,
Controlled for Race (Percentage owning guns)

	White	Black
Region		
Northeast	29.4 (1974)[a]	12.2 (220)
South	62.4 (2415)	56.5 (393)
Midwest	52.8 (1290)	34.1 (205)
West	47.5 (1376)	36.5 (85)
Religion		
Protestant	56.9 (5238)	40.5 (775)
Catholic	37.4 (2194)	20.2 (84)
Jewish	13.1 (285)	—
City Size		
Rural and villages to 2,500	69.8 (2748)	69.4 (186)
Towns 2,500 to 50,000	53.2 (1318)	50.0 (72)
Medium cities 50,000 to 250,000	42.8 (1216)	32.8 (131)
Large cities more than 250,000	30.5 (896)	26.7 (514)

Source: General Social Surveys, 1973, 1974, 1976, 1977 combined.

[a]Raw frequencies indicated in parentheses.

distribution of gun ownership (which is very stable over time) characterizes both races. Southern blacks are more likely to own guns than blacks in the Midwest and West, and the latter are more likely to own guns than blacks in the Northeast. The second section shows that religion is a strong predictor of gun ownership, and that the direction and strength of the relationship is about the same among blacks as among whites. Catholics are much less likely to own guns than Protestants. The final panel shows that exposure to a big city environment decreases the probability of gun ownership among both blacks and whites. The principal reason, then, that black people are less likely to own guns is that they are concentrated in the largest cities.

There is a clear correlation between region and city size (with more northeasterners living in large cities) and between religion and both of these variables (with Catholics and Jews more likely to live in large cities and in the Northeast); therefore, it is conceivable that one or another of these variables explains the others. Further, if we are in fact dealing with historically rooted cultures that are simultaneously defined both regionally and ethnically, then there is no particular reason to expect the variables to combine linearly. It would be quite possible to find, for example, a rural hunting culture among a group of Catholics with a distinctive historical and regional exposure to hunting. Table 31 presents the detailed cross-tabulation of these three variables against gun ownership for whites only, because there are not enough black people even in six studies to use such fine divisions meaningfully.

Table 31. Gun Ownership by Region, Religion, and City Size (Whites Only)
Six Studies from 1959 to 1976 Combined
Percentage owning guns

City size and religion [a]	Region			
	Northeast	South	Midwest	West
Rural and village				
Protestant	63.7 (256)[b]	78.3 (935)	73.2 (695)	69.1 (230)
Catholic	35.8 (179)	56.8 (88)	78.3 (143)	51.7 (60)
Towns from 2,500 to 50,000				
Protestant	39.7 (116)	60.3 (368)	52.4 (334)	65.0 (140)
Catholic	40.2 (122)	45.5 (66)	57.0 (86)	53.8 (26)
Medium city, 50,000 to 250,000				
Protestant	31.6 (117)	52.1 (290)	46.9 (175)	48.4 (159)
Catholic	24.6 (207)	53.3 (45)	46.1 (78)	56.0 (50)
Large city, 250,000 or more				
Protestant	20.5 (229)	51.4 (401)	38.5 (449)	30.9 (337)
Catholic	17.1 (434)	37.2 (94)	32.7 (336)	35.8 (179)
Jewish	11.5 (156)	10.3 (29)	8.8 (34)	8.3 (12)

Source: See Table 30.

[a]Jews living in any but the largest cities are eliminated because there were not enough in any other cell for reliable percentages.

[b]Raw frequencies indicated in parentheses.

First, we see that by and large each of the variables continues to operate even when we control for the others. The percentage of gun owners decreases from rural to urban settings, regardless of religion and race. Second, with a few exceptions, Catholics own fewer guns than Protestants living in the same regions in the same size cities. Finally, with minor exceptions, the South has a greater proportion of gun owners than the Midwest and West (which are about equal), and these regions have a greater proportion of gun owners than the Northeast.

This pattern suggests that a determinant of exposure to the rural culture is the historical moment when a family tradition joined with American history. Most of the people who came to the United States before the middle nineteenth century settled in rural areas, where hunting was a practical and useful pastime. Later immigrant groups entered the social system at the bottom of the urban hierarchy, because the relative size of urban populations grew with industrialization and with the increased efficiency of farming. These later groups were never exposed to the culture that taught hunting skills; besides, it was a good deal harder for them to find a good place to hunt. If this is true, then we should find that more recently arrived ethnic groups should own fewer guns. In the General Social Survey, it is possible to classify those people who give a primary ethnic identification according to the time of the main immigration to the United States. Table 32 presents the results. Clearly earlier immigrants have more guns than later ones.

Table 33 clarifies the sex difference in reporting gun ownership. We see that there is no difference between the reports of men and women when they live in the same household: When a woman reports on a household in which her husband lives, she is as likely to report a gun as is a male respondent. But when we examine households in which no spouse is present, men are very much more likely to report the presence of a gun. Presumably this is because men are generally the owners of guns. (Market research confirms this, placing female ownership at 7 percent of all guns; see Newton and Zimring, 1969).

We have provided support for the argument that gun ownership is distributed as if it were part of a culture that was encouraged in rural, frontier America. Ethnic and religious groups that were more exposed to rural, frontier conditions are more likely to own guns. Frontier traditions are concentrated in more recently settled regions—those regions in which there were greater opportunities to hunt. Males who could participate in that culture are evidently much more likely to own guns.

Table 32. Ethnic Differences in Gun Ownership. Percentage of Gun
Owners Among Respondents Classified According to
the Main Time of Entry of the Ethnic Group
into the United States

Ethnic classification[a]	Percentage owning guns
Old Stock, Whites	57.4 (796)[c]
Unclassifiable and Others, Whites	51.4 (352)
Transition Stock, Whites	48.9 (867)
New Stock, Whites	33.9 (595)
Black[b]	36.1 (332)

Source: General Social Surveys of 1973, 1974, 1976, and 1977.

[a]"Old stock" consists of those giving English, Scottish, Canadian, or Scandinavian origins and those unable to name any country. "Transition stock" is German, Irish, and French. "New stock" is primarily Eastern and Southern European, but also includes Hispanic, Oriental, and others. "Unclassifiable" include those unable to choose a single country and missing cases.

[b]Black people are, of course, "old stock," having "immigrated" almost entirely before the middle of the nineteenth century. However, their entry into the social structure was not such as to encourage gun ownership or free wandering in the forests, so we have separated them here.

[c]Raw frequencies indicated in parentheses.

Table 33. Percentage Owning Guns in Household, by
Sex and Composition of Household

Sex	With spouse	No spouse
Males	55.9 (1009)[a]	43.3 (360)
Females	53.4 (1106)	16.9 (474)

Source: General Social Surveys, 1973, 1974, 1976, and 1977.

[a]Raw frequencies indicated in parentheses.

We have not yet really shown that the frontier culture is indeed a *hunting* culture. Table 34 presents the percentage owning guns in families in which a hunter is present compared with families with no hunters. The weighted average difference between hunters and nonhunters is a hefty 56.8 percent, supporting the relationship between rural, frontier areas and a hunting culture.

Gun Ownership and Punitiveness

The objective distribution of gun ownership appears to be determined by cultural variables combined with opportunities

Table 34. Percentage Owning Guns in Families
with and without Hunters

	Date of study		
	1959	1965	1966
Hunter present	81.7 (569)[a]	87.0 (601)	84.5 (556)
No hunter	30.0 (961)	27.6 (1078)	26.3 (935)

Source: Gallup Polls, 1959, 1965, and 1966.

[a]Raw frequencies indicated in parentheses.

to hunt. If it is true that gun ownership is a cultural response, then there ought to be other cultural attitudes and values that are closely related to gun ownership. In fact, we find that the attitudes central to our earlier analysis of social control are also central in the analysis of the cultural meaning of gun ownership among white people. Table 35 presents the relationship between capital punishment attitudes and gun ownership, controlling for sex and race and also the relationship between wanting harsher courts and gun ownership, again controlling for sex and race.

Table 35. Percentages Favoring Capital Punishment and Wanting Harsher
Courts by Gun Ownership, Sex, and Race

Race,[a] sex, and gun ownership	Favoring capital punishment	Wanting harsher courts[b]
Whites with guns		
Males	80.6 (1280)[c]	87.4 (1123)
Females	68.6 (1202)	88.7 (1075)
Whites without guns		
Males	70.6 (1053)	82.1 (861)
Females	62.9 (1430)	82.8 (1226)
Blacks with guns		
Males	45.9 (109)	77.6 (98)
Females	36.4 (107)	79.8 (94)
Blacks without guns		
Males	46.7 (152)	77.4 (133)
Females	39.1 (230)	82.7 (196)

Source: General Social Surveys, 1973-1974 and 1976-1977 combined.

[a]Races other than black and white are eliminated.

[b]Cases asked a variant form of the courts question in 1974 are eliminated.

[c]Raw frequencies indicated in parentheses.

The first pattern we see is that, among whites, people who own guns are more likely to be punitive. For both sexes and for both dependent variables, the percentage of punitive responses is higher among white people who own guns. Because we have combined four General Social Surveys, these results are statistically significant, even though some of the percentage differences are small. Second, among black people the relationship between gun ownership and punitiveness is substantively quite small and statistically insignificant. Third, if a member of a household reports that there is a gun in the home, this most likely really means that the man of the household owns the gun. We might therefore expect that gun ownership is more strongly correlated with punitive attitudes for men than for women. This result holds for the capital punishment question but not for the courts question.

The overall picture, then, is that among white males, gun ownership is associated with favoring capital punishment and with wanting courts to be harsher with criminals, because the culture of gun ownership was attached to rural places of residence on the nineteenth-century frontiers. This relationship appears to be weaker among women and nonexistent among blacks.

The busing attitude is the one most closely associated with punitiveness (in the range of measures considered in this book); Table 36 tabulates the relationship between gun ownership and views on busing for the 1974 and 1976 General Social

Table 36. Percentage Against Busing,[a] by Gun Ownership and Sex (Whites Only)

Race and gun ownership	Sex	
	Male	Female
Whites		
With guns	89.7 (976)[b]	88.0 (955)
No guns	84.7 (796)	83.2 (1114)

Source: General Social Surveys, 1974 and 1976.

[a]"Don't Know" on busing eliminated.

[b]Raw frequencies indicated in parentheses.

Surveys, which are the only surveys on which these questions occur together. Among whites, the same pattern we have observed with capital punishment attitudes is seen: Gun owners are more likely to oppose busing.

Gun Ownership and Anti-Feminism

The 1974 and 1977 General Social Surveys asked four questions about women's roles that can be related to gun ownership. (The wording for this set of questions can be found in the Appendix under "Feminism.") Hence we can determine whether the sharp sex differentiation of the rural hunting culture is related to a resistance to women leaving traditional feminine roles. The four tabulations are not presented here because none of the differences in sex role attitudes between gun owners and nonowners is significant, even after controlling sex and race; that is, we found no evidence that gun culture is "macho" as well as punitive.

Is Gun Ownership Increasing? In consolidating the data from 1959 to 1976 in order to study regional, religious, and city size effects simultaneously, we took advantage of the fact that the percentage of respondents reporting that they have guns in the household is almost steady. But given the relations established in the section on "The Social Distribution of Gun Ownership," this steadiness of gun ownership is troubling. We have just shown that gun ownership is an element of a cultural complex in which other elements are changing over time, at least since the middle 1960s. But there is no appreciable fluctuation of gun ownership.

All we really know is that there has been no appreciable increase of gun ownership as measured by survey responses. Table 37 presents the best estimates of the number of guns annually entering the market per hundred households. The question before us is whether the rate of sales of guns after 1968 could be nearly double the rate before 1964 without having any effect on the percentage of households with guns. For this to happen, about 3 percent of the families already owning guns would suddenly have to buy an extra gun each

Table 37. Annual Percent Increase in Gun Ownership:
Numbers of Guns[a] Added to Civilian Stock from Production
Plus Imports Minus Exports, 1950-1974, per 100 Households

Year	Armament rate (percentage increase)
1950	5.7
1951	4.7
1952	4.3
1953	4.3
1954	3.4
1955	3.8
1956	4.2
1957	4.0
1958	3.5
1959	4.2
1960	4.1
1961	3.8
1962	3.8
1963	4.0
1964	4.5
1965	5.4
1966	6.0
1967	6.9
1968	8.7
1969	7.0
1970	6.8
1971	7.3
1972	7.8
1973	8.2
1974	9.1

Source: 1950-1968—Newton and Zimring, 1969; 1968-1974—Bureau of Alcohol, Tobacco, and Firearms, n.d.; U.S. Bureau of the Census, 1975, 1976.

[a]The Bureau of Alcohol, Tobacco, and Firearms and the Bureau of the Census disagree on the number of firearms. We have used the Bureau of the Census figures here. See U.S. Congress, 1975, pp. 268-290.

year in the middle 1960s when they had never bought extra guns before that time. Another possibility, obviously, is that the figures from the survey data are inaccurate.

Our argument now requires us to determine whether the survey questions on gun ownership are inaccurate and whether this inaccuracy has been growing over time. The only type of survey error likely to grow systematically over time in response to social forces is intentional deception or intentional non-response, and the only error we can measure is intentional non-response. In the four General Social Surveys with questions on gun ownership (in 1973, 1974, 1976 and 1977), there were only three questions that consistently generated refusals to answer among people who had agreed to the rest of the interview. These were gun ownership, income, and presidential vote. The number of people who refused to answer the gun ownership questions was fifteen in 1973, ten in 1974, seventeen in 1976, and two in 1977. All of these are close enough to 1 percent of total respondents so that this is a reasonable estimate of the error due to intentional nonresponse. Even if all these refusals were gun owners, they could not account for a 3 percent increase in the armament rate per year. What they do indicate is that people may be very sensitive about answering questions about gun ownership and may lie to interviewers (as well as refusing to respond) in order to conceal the fact that they have guns in the house. They may be worried that they should have registered them or that if a strong gun control law were enacted their guns might be confiscated.

We clearly cannot argue that gun ownership has gone up in response to the increase in general punitiveness on the basis that people might possibly be lying to the interviewer on an increasingly large scale. However, a switch in the types of guns owned may give us some insight into the relationship between gun ownership and social control. Long guns such as rifles are designed for hunting, while small guns such as pistols are designed to be carried conveniently in civilian society and are not very successful at killing animals smaller or faster than humans.

Table 38 gives the survey data on the composition of the weaponry owned by those households admitting to gun ownership. The trends over time in this table show a decrease in the percentage of households owning long guns but a steady increase of about .5 percent per year (.46 percent per year weighted estimate of linear change) in the percentage of families owning a pistol. Most of this change is due to an increase of about .33 percent per year in the number of people who own pistols as

Table 38. Breakdown of Gun Owners, by Types of Guns Owned 1959-1976

Gun Owners with:	Date and Survey								
	Gallup 7/59	Gallup 1/65	Gallup 8/66	Gallup 5/72	GSS 3/73	GSS 3/74	GSS 3/76	GSS 3/77
Pistol only	4.5	5.5	4.3	5.9	6.2	6.3	7.7	7.3
Pistol and long	8.4	9.7	11.7	9.9	14.2	13.8	14.3	13.4
Long gun only	35.0	32.7	31.0	27.2	26.7	25.7	24.8	28.5
Total pistols	12.9	15.2	16.0	15.8	20.4	19.1	22.0	20.6
Total long	43.4	42.4	42.7	37.1	40.9	39.5	39.1	41.9
Total gun owners	48.0	47.9	47.0	43.1	47.1	45.9	46.8	49.1

well as long guns. That is, not only is the ownership increasing for guns more oriented toward killing humans but most of that increase is in families whose participation in the rural hunting culture is indicated by owning long guns. The percentage of households owning a pistol only has increased over the period at a rate of about .17 percent per year. The principal change, then, is that fewer people confess to having long guns, and of those who confess to having long guns, a great many more now have pistols as well.

This conclusion is buttressed by the data on further armament. Table 39 gives the percentage of annual additions to the handgun supply. This rose from 24.2 percent during 1899 to 1958 to 47.2 percent in 1968. The 1968 Gun Control Act forced this down to about 34 percent by 1970. From 1970 to 1972, handguns began to recover their share of the supply be-

Table 39. Percentage of Annual Additions to Handgun Supply[a]

Year	Percentage
1899-1958	24.2
1959	29.8
1960	27.9
1961	27.6
1962	29.0
1963	30.3
1964	29.5
1965	32.5
1966	34.4
1967	40.9
1968	47.2
1969	34.8
1970	33.8
1971	36.7
1972	38.9
1973	32.0
1974	33.2

Source: 1950-1968—Newton and Zimring, 1969; 1968-1974—Bureau of Alcohol, Tobacco, and Firearms, n.d.; U.S. Bureau of the Census, 1975, 1976.

[a]The Bureau of Alcohol, Tobacco, and Firearms and the Bureau of the Census disagree on the number of firearms. Where there was disagreement, we have used Bureau of the Census figures.

fore slumping to a ten-year low in 1973-1974. Obviously the figures show the rising supply of handguns that would be expected to accompany a rise in the ownership of this type of weapon.

Combined, then, these data suggest that there may indeed have been a sudden increase of around 3 percent in the middle 1960s in purchases of new guns by families who already owned guns. Although it is questionable whether the number of families with long guns actually decreased, it is more certain that the increase in pistol-owning families came mainly from hunting families. This addition of armaments directed mainly toward humans by families who already owned guns directed mainly toward animals may, then, have been a social control response among people whom we have shown to be more punitive in their social control attitudes. The increase in pistol ownership and in the number of guns in circulation per capita, therefore, probably had the same significance as the increases observed during the same period in favoring capital punishment and harsher criminal courts.

Fear, Neighborhood, and Support for Gun Registration

We showed in Chapter Three that people who own guns are considerably less afraid to walk near their homes at night, but this was almost entirely due to the fact that people who own guns live in different size cities and in different kinds of neighborhoods than those who do not own guns. Table 40 shows a related trend—that there is much less support for gun registration among people who own guns. The weighted average difference in support for gun registration between gun owners and nonowners is 22.2 percent. There will probably be a spurious relation between fear and attitude toward gun control legislation, then, because gun owners live in places where people are less likely to be afraid and because gun owners oppose gun registration. Consequently, people who are not afraid will oppose gun registration even if there is no causal relation between fear of crime and gun control attitudes.

Table 41 shows the percentage favoring gun registration

Table 40. Percentage Favoring Gun Registration
by Gun Ownership, 1959-1977

	Gun ownership	
Date	Own gun	No gun
1959	68.8 (721)[a]	86.6 (752)
1965	62.0 (792)	88.0 (836)
1966	56.8 (701)	81.1 (763)
1973	63.7 (692)	85.9 (754)
1974	65.5 (675)	86.1 (772)
1976	60.2 (686)	84.3 (764)
1977	62.5 (757)	84.2 (733)

Source: Gallup Polls, 1959, 1965, and 1966; General Social Surveys, 1973-1974 and 1976-1977.

[a]Raw frequencies indicated in parentheses.

Table 41. Percentage Favoring Gun Registration, by Fear and Sex
(Whites Only)

	Fear	
Sex and Years	Yes	No
1967		
Males	76.5 (102)[a]	63.0 (602)
Females	85.3 (306)	82.5 (394)
1973-1974		
Males	76.7 (240)	64.4 (964)
Females	84.2 (805)	80.0 (536)
1976-1977		
Males	72.0 (261)	59.9 (933)
Females	82.2 (880)	75.2 (568)

Source: Gallup Poll, 1967, General Social Surveys, 1973-1974 combined and 1976-1977 combined.

[a]Raw frequencies indicated in parentheses.

by fear, controlling for sex, in 1967 and 1973-1974. We see that fear makes more difference in support for gun registration for males than for females (this difference for males is significant). But we have argued that this result might be spurious, and the fact that the relationship is stronger among males, who are likely to be the effective owners of guns, increases this liklihood.

Table 42 therefore controls for gun ownership in correlating fear and support for gun control. Except among women in families with no guns (who support gun control at the 90 percent level whether they are afraid of crime or not), there

Table 42. Percentage Favoring Gun Registration, by Fear, Sex, and Gun
Ownership (Whites Only)

Sex and gun ownership	Fear	
	Yes	No
Males		
With gun	60.7 (224)[a]	51.7 (1080)
No gun	86.3 (271)	77.6 (793)
Females		
With gun	73.9 (706)	67.6 (552)
No gun	90.4 (964)	88.0 (540)

Source: General Social Surveys, 1973-1974 and 1976-1977.

[a]Raw frequencies indicated in parentheses.

remains a strong relationship between fear and gun control
attitudes even after controlling for the spurious influence of
gun ownership.

Trends in Behavior and Attitudes Toward Firearms

The remaining issue to explore is the lack of any trend
in gun control attitudes. If the increase in punitiveness toward
criminals is, in some sense, an attempt by the public to solve
the problem of increased violent crime, then why does this
increased concern not result in increased support for preventive
as well as punitive measures?

Our argument here is that fear of crime does indeed increase people's support for gun control, making perhaps as
much as a ten percentage point difference. However those
parts of the population that were most fearful or where fear
increased most—women, urban dwellers, those who did not
own guns—were practically unanimous in supporting gun
registration even before the increase in crime rates. When the
percentage endorsing a public policy reaches the level of 90
percent, it is unlikely that any cause operating over time will
push it much higher. Consequently we must turn our attention
to men and to people in small cities, who have some room to
move to higher levels of endorsement. In particular, we have to
pay attention to gun owners, who constitute most of the opposition to gun control.

This brings up the knotty problem that gun control, unlike tough courts and capital punishment, is not a measure tailored to fit known criminals but a general measure affecting all gun owners or potential owners. In particular it touches members of a distinctive rural hunting culture. One characteristic of this culture is support for gun ownership and opposition to gun control. Members of this culture are more likely to live in areas of low fear and low victimization, but, ironically, another characteristic of this culture is a relatively more punitive notion of how to control crime. What appears to have happened is that the gun-owning and nonowning cultures have moved in opposite directions when confronted with the rise in violent crime. By and large the response of gun owners was to buy pistols; that of nonowners was to demand that pistols be registered.

Neither of the forces for change in gun control attitudes has been terribly strong. The moderate relation between fear and favoring gun control (or between neighborhood type and favoring gun control) could not have had a very strong effect on gun control attitudes over time, because the people who were increasing most in fear were already preponderantly in favor of gun control. The response of buying pistols occurred among people who were already greatly inclined to treat the crime problem with harsher punishment rather than gun control.

The issue of gun control tends to split the country repeatedly along the same lines, with almost the same distribution of public opinion in each district at each point in time. Unlike the steady recent evolution of public opinion on capital punishment or the increasing similarity of women to men on the court severity questions, federal gun regulation breaks the country up into the same units now that it did two decades ago: the rural South, Midwest, and West versus the urban Northeast at the extremes, with the urban South, Midwest, and West and the small-town Northeast in between. As we have shown in Chapter Three, the recent crime problem has not hit regions of the rural hunting culture as hard as it has hit other places. In other words, the crime problem has been concentrated among people who were already in favor of gun control. Therefore, the increase in crime has not changed the structure of public opinion on gun control.

6

Sources of Public Support for Harsher Penalties

. . . .
. . . .
. . . .

Opinions About Crime and Punishment

We have noted that victimization, fear of crime, and support for harsher penalties have all increased in the past two decades. At first it seemed reasonable that these trends were directly related at the individual level—that punishment was seen as a pragmatic solution to the problem of crime. In fact, our data show that support for harsher treatment of criminals is not related to any of our measures of salience (see Tables 21-24).

One could argue that there are pragmatic solutions to some of the problems posed by increased crime. People may decide, for instance, that the way to protect themselves from crime in their neighborhoods is to stay indoors at night. In this context, being afraid of walking alone on dark streets is a preparation for the pragmatist solution of not giving the muggers a chance. It could be that the lower victimization rate for women is due to the fact that this pragmatic strategy works rather well. If so, increased salience of crime results in the increased likelihood of using a rational solution to reduce the risks of victimization.

The issue of what to do about criminals once they have committed crimes is more complicated. Compared with the sensible reaction one may have to the risks on neighborhood streets (staying indoors, walking with other people at night), increasing the punishment for convicted criminals is a rather indirect solution. Changing the cost-benefit function for crimes of various sorts is only a pragmatic solution to the extent that it really deters crime. As Zimring and Hawkins (1973) have noted, it is very difficult to tell how well punishment actually works as a deterrent. Therefore, locking the doors and staying at home at night may be direct results of the increased salience of crime, because they are actions that reduce the probability of victimization. There is a weaker empirical and logical connection between fear and victimization on one hand and fear and support for harsher penalties on the other. Therefore, we would expect that the correlations at the individual level between these measures would not be significant.

As we have seen, individuals who are afraid are no more likely to support harsher sanctions than individuals for whom crime is a less salient problem (Tables 21 and 22). In addition, we will also see that individuals who have been victimized or who live in high-crime areas are no more likely to support punitive measures than more fortunate individuals. We do, however, find some effect of salience of crime on public opinion about punishment. People who live in high-crime areas are more likely to have logically consistent "ideological" responses to the crime problem. In other words, we find increased cognitive consistency in areas where crime is more salient.

The "cognitive consistency approach" to public opinion research (see Converse, 1964) argues that people develop coherent ideologies in situations of increased salience. When issues become salient, people think more about them. This results in the acceleration of the process by which people develop world views—consistent sets of propositions about how the world works. On any given question of a liberal-conservative kind, for instance, an increase in salience is likely to push liberals toward a more uniform liberal response and encourage conservatives to more consistently respond conservatively. The main effect of increased salience, in the cognitive consistency approach to opinion research, is increased ideological consistency. An ideological position simplifies responses to complexes of problems, because it offers the basis for a ritualized response.

Our first conclusion in this chapter is that the correlation among punitive attitudes is stronger for people who are in the *social* (but not personal) circumstance of increased salience. Chapter Four outlined the basis for including punitive attitudes in the complex of beliefs comprising the tradition of American liberalism. The second finding in this chapter is that the liberal complex is more highly integrated in social circumstances (that is, neighborhoods) where crime is more salient. Finally, Chapter Four also examined the relation between punitive attitudes and support for busing. The third finding in this chapter is that the causes of consistency between these two issues operate with greater force in social circumstances where crime is more salient.

Figure 4. Interrelationship of Variables in Chapter Six

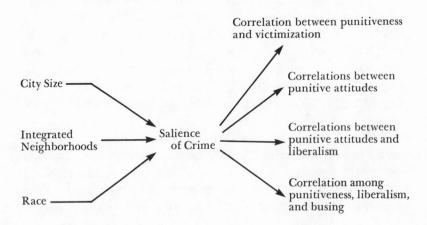

Although we expect that rational or pragmatic theories of public opinion will apply to blacks as well as to whites, it is clear that the process of attitude formation on the issue of punishment of criminals ought to be quite different for the two groups. Capital punishment was once abolished by the courts primarily because it was shown to be discriminatory against blacks and the poor; naturally such evidence might cause blacks to take a dimmer view of capital punishment. They might also be expected to be more generally suspicious of a court system that has been shown to discriminate against blacks in the severity of punishment. In fact, we find these expectations to be correct: blacks and whites have quite different relations to the criminal justice system. Blacks are more likely to have experienced first hand a strict law-and-order regime, and in this context, the reluctance of blacks to endorse harsh social control measures is a rational response.

In addition to this difference in levels of support for punitive solutions to the crime problem, a difference is also found in the ideological context of social control and related attitudes. When we consider cognitive consistency among blacks and whites, we should realize that questions about race relations may be a part of a tolerance complex among whites but connected to a self-interest complex for blacks. We therefore find that "liberalism" sometimes means different things to blacks than to whites and that the intercorrelations among the relevant items are not the same for the two groups.

Explaining Punitive Ideology

In Chapter Three, we examined fear and the "most important problem" question in an attempt to explain the level of support for harsher punishment of criminals. We observed results that did not coincide with our intuitive beliefs about the issue. For both whites and blacks, we found that there was no relationship between the salience of crime (determined by fear of walking alone or by listing crime as the most important national problem) and support for capital punishment or demanding harsher courts (see Tables 21-24). Table 43 shows the pattern of punitive responses when whites and blacks are classified by whether or not they report a recent victimization. There is a significant relationship among whites between victimization and support for harsher sanctions, but it is in the opposite direction from what we would expect under the original hypothesis about the relation between salience and opinion. Whites whose homes have been recently burglarized are less likely than those with no victimization experience to favor capital punishment and less likely to demand harsher courts. There is no significant relationship for blacks, which is at least consistent with the lack of relationship reported in Chapter Three.

Table 43. The Relationship between Victimization and Punitive Attitudes
(in Percentages)

	Ever burglarized	
	Yes	No
Whites		
Supporting capital punishment	60.7 (321)[a]	71.7 (4512)
Demanding harsher courts	79.2 (269)	85.9 (3919)
Blacks		
Supporting capital punishment	51.2 (84)	46.6 (704)
Demanding harsher courts	79.4 (68)	80.8 (604)

Source: General Social Surveys, 1972-1978; also reported in Taylor and others, 1979.

[a]Raw frequencies indicated in parentheses.

The cognitive consistency theory gives us another opportunity to examine the effect of salience on support for harsher punishment. To do this, we examine the relationships among punitive attitudes—and between these punitive attitudes and the value premises associated with them—for people with differential exposure to the problem of crime and victimization. One way to do this is to examine the relationships between punitive attitudes of those who have been victimized and those who have not. A second way is to examine the structure of punitive attitudes of people who live in environments that differ in the salience of the crime problem. The cognitive consistency theory of public opinion predicts that those for whom the issue of crime is salient will have a more consistent and more coherent understanding of the problem and their relation to it. Specifically, this means that the intercorrelations among punitive attitudes will be stronger for those who have been victimized and/or live in areas of high victimization.

People's levels of fear of crime and their victimization experience are measures of the personal salience of the crime problem to them. The cognitive consistency theory of public opinion tells us that people organize their beliefs more consistently when they are subject to greater pressure to solve problems. But the theory does not specify the cues that comprise this pressure. If consistent attitudes are the result of localized personal experiences (such as being robbed), then the more consistent structure of public opinion that results from increased salience is somehow peculiar to the specific variations in the biographies of individual people. If, however, people respond to cues in the environment—basing their judgments on the widespread belief that certain areas of the city have a bad reputation or on the public knowledge of the higher risks of victimization in certain neighborhoods—then it is also likely that they rely on other sources of public information such as media or public addresses for "packaging" their beliefs. To the extent that people rely on public information and public leaders for opinion leadership, they are responding to social cues. Geographic areas with more public attention to the crime issue are areas of increased social salience. By identifying people according to their individual experiences of crime (fear and victimization), we are differentiating according to the personal salience of the crime problem. When we identify according to the geographic place of residence, we separate the population according to the social salience of the crime problem in one's environment. (A similar analysis of the importance of information and leadership in the packaging of political beliefs was made by Nie, Verba, and Petrocik, 1976).

We will first examine the relationship between personal experience and consistency of attitudes. Table 44 shows the intercorrelations (Yule's Q) between support for capital punishment, demand for harsher courts, and self-ascribed political

views, with "conservative" scored as the positive direction
(see the Appendix for exact wordings) for whites who have
different personal victimization experiences or who are differentially fearful. If consistency is the result of personal salience,
the intercorrelations should be higher for those who have been
victimized and for those who are afraid. In all but one case the
pattern is in the wrong direction; that is, individuals with no
personal victimization are slightly more consistent in their
views. The one difference that is in the right direction—the correlation between support for capital punishment and demand
for harsher courts is higher for those who are afraid than for
those who are not—is a very small effect and not statistically
significant. The conclusion to be drawn from Table 44 is that
fear and actual victimization, while they represent increases in
the personal salience of crime, do not produce more consistent
ideological approaches to prescribing harsh treatment for
criminals.

Table 44. Intercorrelations Between Punitive Attitudes for Whites With
Different Levels of Personal Salience of Fear and Victimization
(Yule's Q)

	Level of fear		Ever burglarized	
	Afraid	Not afraid	Yes	No
Support capital punishment X Demand harsher courts	.62	.58	.50	.60
Support capital punishment X Conservative political views	.37	.41	.27	.41
Demand harsher courts X Conservative political views	.21	.46	.18	.38

Source: General Social Surveys, 1972-1978; also reported in Taylor and
others, 1979.

To study the social salience of the crime problem, we
looked at respondents who lived in neighborhoods that differed
in the level of fear of crime and reported risks of victimization.

Precinct or block statistics were not available to link neighborhood characteristics directly to each respondent's record, so
it was necessary to use surrogate measures to describe the type
of neighborhood in which each respondent lived. To examine
the effect of social salience, we used the typology of white
neighborhoods described in Chapter Three. The typology
differentiates size of place and integrated versus segregated
neighborhood status.

Before proceeding, we should justify this choice as a
measure of social salience. The issue of crime, race, and segregation are currently intertwined in American society (Wolfgang
and Cohen, 1970). Without attempting a full explanation, we
note that whites who live in areas where blacks also live are
usually more likely to be exposed to certain kinds of victimization. In this sense proximity to blacks is a measure of the social
salience of the crime problem. The cause of this is embedded in
a much larger web of social processes that shape American
urban life. A broader, comparative view of urban life is that
blacks are now the predominant inhabitants of the areas of the
city where crime has historically been the greatest, regardless
of the ethnic composition of the inhabitants (Shaw and McKay,
1942; Wilks, 1967). Therefore, whites who live near blacks are
more likely to live near these areas. The measure of neighborhood integration is, therefore, a measure of proximity to areas
of the city where crime rates are historically high. It is the
area of the city where blacks reside and not the blacks themselves that makes the neighborhood integration a measure of
the salience of crime.

Our classification of neighborhoods of white respondents
yields a 3 by 2 typology: small, medium sized, and large communities of residence by segregated or integrated neighborhood
status. Chapter Three describes the great variation in rates of
fear and victimization within categories of the typology (see
Tables 12-14). To summarize, each step up in the size-of-place
classification produces an increase in both the level of fear and
the level of victimization. For any given size of place, whites
who live in integrated neighborhoods are more afraid than

whites who live in segregated neighborhoods and are also more likely to report having been victimized. It is interesting to note that although the rates for blacks are high, they are not as high as for whites living in integrated neighborhoods in large cities. This is because the majority of blacks do not live in the largest cities and so are subject to lower "environmental" rates of victimization than the most victimized category of the white population.

The six kinds of neighborhoods (three sizes times two racial mixtures) shown in Table 45 vary greatly in the social salience of the crime problem. The simplest theory of public opinion, which we are calling the pragmatist theory, predicts that the level of support for harsher punishment should be higher in areas where there is higher victimization. The data once again contradict the pragmatist theory: There are no differences between the neighborhoods in the overall level of support for capital punishment and in the demand for harsher courts. (The percentages are shown in the rows of the table labeled "% Overall level of support.") The lack of any pattern is surprising. Environmental areas that differ greatly in the levels of fear and victimization do not differ in the level of support for harsher punishment.

Table 45 supports the cognitive consistency theory quite clearly. The correlations between the attitude measures usually increase with size of place and, for any given size of place, are usually higher in integrated than in segregated neighborhoods. The intercorrelations for blacks are all substantially lower and not at all commensurate with their aggregate levels of fear and victimization. Even though there is some tendency for the structure of opinions to be similar for blacks and whites (the signs of the relationships all agree), it is clear that the issues mean quite different things to the black population than to the white population.

The pattern of results reported here and in table 46 could be a spurious result of higher levels of education in larger cities and in integrated neighborhoods. To test this possibility, the analyses were run separately within educational levels. The results still support the consistency theory. There is an *additional* educational effect on ideology: Within all neighborhood types, the intercorrelations among attitudes are higher for those with more education. Similarly, within educational groups, the intercorrelations are lower for blacks, so the pattern of racial differences is not due to educational inequality. These results are consistent with most of the other research on the effects of education on attitude consistency.

Busing in Relation to Salience of Crime

We have shown in several ways that, in the cross-section, salience of crime in one's personal experience does not have a great deal to do with one's level of support for harsher sanctions. Social (environmental) salience, however, makes a great deal of difference, not so much in the level of punitiveness as in the way people think about the problems of crime and punishment. In areas where the problem is more salient, people have a more coherent point of view on the problem, involving other values and political beliefs (such as liberalism) in addition to opinions on the issue of crime itself.

What cues do people respond to in developing coherent ideologies? Our analysis of the effects of personal victimization suggests that it is unlikely that a person develops a systematic pattern of beliefs because of personal experiences alone; it is more likely that there is a process of mutual reinforcement between environmental cues, public sources of information (such as newspapers, political leaders, and community crime-prevention programs), and personal experience. The major political implication of this finding is that once an ideology about crime and punishment exists, new social issues that have relatively little to do with the punishment of criminals can become part of the old complex. The integration of a new social issue into an old ideological framework brings it into an already established pattern of community conflict. As we noted in Chapter Four, this happened with the issue of busing. Support for busing to achieve racial balance is only weakly related to the traditional measures of racial tolerance, but opposition to busing is strongly related to support for capital punishment and the demand for harsher courts (see Tables 28 and 29). Busing

Table 45. Neighborhood Differences in Intercorrelations Between Punitive Attitudes (Yule's Q)

	Size of place of residence		
	Less than 10,000	10,000-250,000	Larger than 250,000
Whites in segregated neighborhoods			
Support capital punishment X Demand harsher courts	.45	.60	.71
Support capital punishment X Conservative political views	.18	.41	.48
Demand harsher courts X Conservative political views	.30	.45	.34
% Overall level of support:			
Capital punishment	69	71	70
Harsher courts	87	85	87
Whites in integrated neighborhoods			
Support capital punishment X Demand harsher courts	.70	.65	.74
Support capital punishment X Conservative political views	.30	.49	.50

Demand harsher courts X Conservative political views	.22	.26	.39
% Overall level of support:			
Capital punishment	73	70	63
Harsher courts	85	85	84

Blacks combining all size categories

Support capital punishment X Demand harsher courts	.59
Support capital punishment X Conservative political views	.17
Demand harsher courts X Conservative political views	.11
% Overall level of support:	
Capital punishment	46
Harsher courts	76

Source: General Social Surveys, 1972-1978; also reported in Taylor, Scheppele, and Stinchcombe, 1979.

is linked in the public mind to the growing ideology about crime and appropriate treatment of criminals and is therefore unlikely to be understood in terms of the traditional individual (and social) commitments to racial equality and integration.

Neighborhood types do not differ on the level of support for busing. Busing attitudes are also unrelated to the personal salience of crime. The correlations between fear of crime or victimization and support for busing are all small and statistically insignificant. The environmental salience of crime, as measured by the neighborhood typology, however, has a great deal to do with the relationship between busing attitudes and support for harsher criminal sanctions. Table 46 shows the correlations within each type of neighborhood between support for busing and the three other opinion measures considered earlier—support for capital punishment, demand for harsher courts, and self-ascribed political liberalism.

The pattern is clear-cut: The relationship between opposition to busing and punitive ideology about crime and crime prevention depends on the social salience of the crime issue. In areas where fear and victimization are salient issues, people develop more consistent ideological points of view. In these more dangerous areas, busing for racial balance is more likely to be associated with the same set of issues and thus re-create those divisions of the community originally caused by the crime problem. The deeper psychological connections between busing and the crime issue have been analyzed at great length in Chapter Four. What we have added to that discussion is the observation that the forces producing a coherent public ideology regarding criminal sanctions and the forces relating this ideology to public opinion on crime are much stronger and much more clearly defined in geographical areas where crime and "forced busing" are extremely salient public issues.

Table 46. Neighborhood Differences in Intercorrelations Between Punitive Attitudes and Support for Busing (Yule's Q)

	Size of place of residence		
	Less than 10,000	10,000-250,000	Larger than 250,000
Whites in segregated neighborhoods			
Oppose busing X Capital punishment	.24	.30	.50
Oppose busing X Harsher courts	.15	.39	.59
Oppose busing X Political conservation	.20	.33	.41
% Overall level of opposition:	86	86	88
Busing for racial balance			
Whites in integrated neighborhoods			
Oppose busing X Capital Punishment	.36	.42	.49
Oppose busing X Harsher courts	.27	.51	.53
Oppose busing X Political conservation	.22	.34	.55
% Overall level of opposition:			
Busing for racial balance	89	84	82
Blacks combining all size categories			
Oppose busing X Capital punishment	.20		
Oppose busing X Harsher courts	.21		
Oppose busing X Political conservatism	.19		
% Overall level of opposition:	55		
Busing for racial balance			

Source: General Social Surveys, 1972-1978; also reported in Taylor, Scheppele, and Stinchcombe, 1979.

7

Implications for Public Policy

. . . .
. . . .
. . . .

The significance of this book lies in its adding a national dimension to research on public reactions to crime and punishment in American society. This area of research is usually the concern of urban sociology, and the people who devote detailed attention to it often focus on large cities—and sometimes only those areas of large cities that are integrated or black. As a consequence, most of the "common knowledge" about crime and punishment is knowledge about the social processes of large, racially mixed urban areas. But we have learned (for instance, in the case of gun control) that the policy process—and even the contours of national trends in policy preference—can be substantially altered by the input of nonurban areas as well. Many of the empirical surprises and much of the refashioning of the common knowledge about crime and punishment in this book result from our including in the analysis racially mixed urban areas and other areas of the country, in proportion to the weight each area has in national rates of victimization, fear, and support for changes in national policy.

136

When we pool the results for the entire national population, we find that the actuarial probabilities of victimization—particularly of the most fearful kind of victimization—are quite low. The high aggregate social cost from violent criminal victimization experiences stems from the fact that a low probability event (violent victimization) is multiplied by a tremendously high personal cost (physical, psychological, and financial). When confronted with this situation, the personal and policy alternatives are to try to lower the probabilities of encounter even further and to compensate the damages. The pursuit of these responses to crime multiplies the personal costs of actual victimization into a tremendously high aggregate social cost. In this sense, our study could be subtitled "Crimeless Victims."

The actions we routinely take, both individually and collectively, to lower the probabilities of victimization—for instance the proliferation of controlled access security systems or the use of streetlights so bright that the trees can no longer distinguish the seasons of the year—also make the environment less pleasant to live in. At one time the dream of the urban dweller was to escape the sounds of traffic and industry; now the goal is as much to escape the omnipresent electronic eye. Preventive actions not only lower the quality of life but also serve as constant reminders of the reasons for their existence. Therefore a slight increase in the rate of victimization—or even, we suspect, in the rate of preventive action alone—produces a rapid and much greater inflation in the subjective probabilities and percentage of people fearful of crime. This is the second sense in which the public is victimized even though the average individual is not. The third harm to the public is financial: Each of us bears part of the cost of policing, other preventive activities, and of victim restitution.

The principal intellectual puzzle of this book stems from the mismatch between the personal variables that constitute the policy problems of crime control (that is, fear and victimization) and the opinion measures that constitute demands on the political system (attitudes toward the courts, capital punishment, and gun control). The individual harms of victimization are highly concentrated by social group and within

geographical areas. The collective harms, such as fear or awareness of the crime problem, are somewhat more evenly distributed. However, demands for local improvement or change in
the judicial system are nearly uniformly distributed across all
categories of the population. The result is that fairly uniform
pressure in public opinion is brought to bear on policy makers
to solve what is actually an extremely localized problem. Unless some adjustment is made in matching remedial actions and
remedial resources to areas of greatest objective need, a policy
process that allocates resources according to the level of public
demand will result in an unfair distribution of attention. Public
awareness of the priorities for remedial action and the policy
process in crime control in general are topics beyond the scope
of this book. What we have done is provide a fairly detailed
springboard for these studies.

The organization of the book shows that different sub-
jects in the general area of attitudes toward crime and punishment require different units of analysis and different modes of
approaching the problem. Chapter Two tells us what we might
determine about crime and punishment from trends over time.
The units of analysis were therefore years, usually yearly
measurements on the country as a whole.

Chapter Three focused on the actuarial variables of fear.
We asked what determines the risk of victimization, the vulnerability to substantial loss, and the incapacity to take any pro-
tective measures. The units of analysis were situations in which
people live and the features of those situations that increase
or decrease various probabilities of damage. We also examined
the relationship between salience (as measured by fear and the
nation's most important problem) and punitiveness. People's
levels of fear seem to be determined by their "small environments"—their neighborhoods, their family and household com-
positions, their sex, and whether they walk on the streets at
night. Except insofar as social characteristics determine whether
people live in high-risk environments, there is very little evidence that fear of crime is part of a general world view or
cultural tradition. Consequently we must analyze fear and
victimization with variables that differentiate the population

according to levels of risk and vulnerability—the probabilities that they will be defenseless when confronted with a threat of violence and that they will have a lot to lose in that encounter.

In Chapter Four we turned to individual psyches and the interrelationships among attitudes within them. At issue was the extent to which attitudes toward punishment constitute parts of a general world view about public policy—either a liberal Enlightenment view or a conservative law-and-order view. The units of analysis were therefore attitude complexes in individual people. While attitudes toward crime and punishment are to some extent the outcome of fear and of believing that crime is an important public policy problem, they are also part of liberal and law-and-order world views. This fact becomes especially interesting in light of the fact that liberal world views have become more prevalent while superficially contradictory punitive attitudes have also become more prevalent in the same time and place. But the fundamental variables involved are those in the biographies of individuals that produce one or another kind of world view, and the central subject of study is how to bring attitudes into compatibility with individuals.

Although we explored the coherence of the liberal world view through the history of political ideas stemming from the Enlightenment, the central data base consists of relations among attitudes in the cross-section—that is, how much relationship is there between civil liberties attitudes and attitudes toward punishment of criminals? It is important that the same Bill of Rights that guarantees freedom of speech also prohibits cruel and unusual punishment; however, the crucial question for us is what accounts for their still having some cross-sectional correlation in the 1970s. Thus, even though the elements of our analysis are part of a cultural tradition the units on which we actually measure world views are individuals; the theory that connects attitudes toward punishment of criminals to attitudes toward civil liberties (or toward sex, abortion, and women's roles) is a theory that applies to individuals.

In Chapter Five we discussed gun control attitudes in terms of gun ownership, having found that gun ownership is the principal determinant of gun control attitudes. Our central observation is that gun ownership can serve as a tracer for the location of a male rural hunting culture. By using that tracer we find that male hunters tend to be Protestants or rural Catholics, that they tend to live especially in the South but also in the Midwest and West, that (other things being equal) they tend to be earlier immigrants into the United States (except for blacks). Ultimately, we found that there is no complicated process of ideological congruence to study; rather, the matter is simply one of "social geography," of describing empirically the regions and ethnicities and sexes within which this culture of gun ownership is found. Although the units in the tables are, of course, individual people, the variables at the heads and sides of the tables are measures of exposure to the rural hunting cultural complex. So the real operative variable is a cultural tradition, which we examine by studying differences in exposure to it.

Finally in Chapter Six the unit of analysis is the neighborhood. We wanted to study the effects of fear on public opinion, and our desire to do so was reinforced by the contrasting results of the time series for the collectivity in Chapter Two and the individual analyses in Chapters Three, Four, and Five. We needed to find a collectivity that varied in its general exposure to fear-producing crime. We know from Chapter Three that neighborhoods are collectivities that vary in exposure to fear-producing crime and that neighborhoods in large cities in integrated settings or ghetto settings are exposed to higher crime rates than rural areas in about the same proportion as recent American crime rates are higher than American crime rates a decade ago. The question, then, is whether the dynamics of public opinion formation in the central city are similar to the dynamics of public opinion formation in the central city are similar to the dynamics of opinion formation in recent times because they are both exposed to high rates of fear-producing crime. The answer is they are not. The relations between ideas that constitute "common knowledge" about crime, punishment, and related measures are quite different in large, racially mixed urban areas than in other parts of the country.

On Public Opinion Theory and Research

In explaining the connections between the findings in each chapter, we have relied on certain key premises of social psychological research. The lack of a well-developed theory of public opinion did not present much of a stumbling block for the initial chapter drafts but became increasingly problematic as we reconciled one set of findings with another. In refining our insights into public opinion, we invoked several explanatory principles. We view these as brief excursions on mechanisms that might explain what is going on rather than grand theoretical generalizations. The explanatory mechanisms most often invoked to show what direction theory might go (and consequently what additional data might need to be generated) are *attribution*—the development of ideas about the causes and effects of things in public opinion—and *salience*.

Attribution. Let us consider a simple example: a gun owner does not believe that registering himself and other gun-owners in rural areas will solve the crime problem concentrated in the central parts of the largest cities where relatively few people own guns. Clearly the reason he (the respondent is usually male) does not make the connection between registering guns and the reduction of crime is that he has fairly good opposing evidence: he himself and most other gun owners use guns to kill pheasants, ducks, and deer rather than people. To this respondent, gun owners are not an abstract category that might as well be registered in case it does some good; rather, they are specific people about whose criminal intent he can make a good judgment. Crime does not move him toward gun registration because he does not attribute the cause of the trouble to gun owners.

Similarly let us suppose the truth of our argument that judgments on busing, harsher courts, and capital punishment are all judgments about how much we can trust courts to solve social problems—specifically problems of the ghetto. We postulated that people differ in their judgments of where the bad effects of the ghetto come from, and of how powerful courts and school systems are as controls of those evil effects. The argument was therefore about attributing causal efficacy or power to courts and laws.

The intervening links between general liberalism and lenience likewise consist of elements such as respondents' judgments of the probability that innocent people will be convicted, of whether mitigating circumstances are likely, of whether the distribution of penalties is prejudiced, and so on. That is, we argued that punitive attitudes are connected to a conservative world view and lenient attitudes to a liberal world view because the world views affect the way that a person will view the "average crime" he or she is asked to think about on the harsher courts question, or the "average murder" on the capital punishment question.

The intervening mechanisms we have introduced to account for troubling correlations (or troubling lack of correlations) are typically speculations about the attributions of causal efficacy, of responsibility and guilt, of the effects of some institution or of some public policy, or of the character of some person described by an abstract social category. Our problem then is that we do not have measures of these intervening processes. For example, we do not know whether rural men would respond differently from urban women to the statement, "The average person I have met (or would be likely to meet) carrying a gun was up to no good"; or whether blacks and whites differ in answer to, "Most punishments fit the crime fairly well regardless of race or poverty"; or whether liberals differ from conservatives on, "Courts usually differ with public opinion only when there are important constitutional values at stake." That is, we do not have the required subtlety of measures of the total mode of thought about crime and punishment, about guns and punishment, about courts and punishment, that would be required to study the mechanisms we have been tempted to postulate.

Heise (1969, 1977) has shown that the reaction to simple sentences and to the objects and actions within those sentences is strongly affected by reactions to the other elements in the sentences. For example, the average valuation of *uncle* in a neutral sentence is .99 (somewhat positive), but is 1.80 (very positive) in the sentence "The uncle helped the father" (1969, p. 207). If, over a historical period, the average valuation of *father* changes, Heise's argument holds that the valuation of *uncle* in that sentence would also change. Similarly, in the sentence, "Do you favor capital punishment for a person convicted of murder?" a change in the perception of whether the average murderer is a jealous husband or a ruthless robber ought to change the valuation of capital punishment in the sentence.

Presumably the simple attitude questions we have been dealing with encourage people to fill in their current average attributions (average goodness, average powerfulness, average level of activity) for the objects in the sentence. That is, the question on harsher courts encourages people to fill in their picture of the average court, the average crime, the average criminals, and perhaps the average victim and to make an overall judgment. If, over time, the average court comes to be seen as interfering with the just punishment of bad criminals, powerless against crime in the ghetto, and inconsiderate of innocent victimized women, we will expect disapproval of the court's actions. In contrast, if the perception of the average criminal changes over time from a too highly spirited boy down the block to a dangerous young black man with a gun, the appropriateness of harsher punishments might increase.

The point is that if we knew all these aspects of a situation and had measures of what the respondent thought was "normal," we could trace the movement of each of those aspects over time and explain trends and correlations. Because we do not have this rich map of the cognitive content of these attitudes, our trends go in one direction and our correlations in another. As an example, let us consider our two contrary hypotheses about the harsher courts question. One states that people generally perceive correctly that the days spent in prison per violent crime known to the police is decreasing and that they believe this is due to the growing lenience of the courts. The other states that people want more punishment now than earlier because they believe the crime problem now is more serious than before. If we had a qualitative account in their own

words of why they believe courts should be harsher or what
they believe capital punishment would accomplish—taken at both
points in time and then coded for perception of weak courts
and for mentions of rising crime rates—we could determine
which theory of attribution of the causes of inadequate punishments had the most weight. Further, if we had scales of perceived punitiveness and strength of the courts, the perceived
average penalty per crime, and the perceived seriousness of the
crime problem, we would at least be able to weight changes in
these variables as determinants of increased punitive answers. In
the absence of such tools, our measures of salience do not correlate at all strongly with punitive responses, and we do not know.

   Salience. From one point of view, the central variable in
this book is the salience of the crime problem: Fear, victimization, the lack of neighborhood safety, and seeing crime as a
national problem are all measures of salience. These in turn
might (1) lead to increases in punitiveness and in support for
gun control, (2) dissociate lenience toward criminals from a
general liberal world view so that the two could move in opposite
directions, or (3) cause increased cognitive consistency.

   It is a common theory in the social sciences, that "increased strain" has predictable consequences for public opinion
and other collective behavior (Smelser, 1962). We have not had
much luck with this theory, however. The effects of differences
among people in the degree of salience of crime (as measured by
fear and seeing crime as a national problem) were not very large,
although they were in the right direction to explain the trend.
However, when we measured variations in salience across neighborhoods, we found that the more fear-ridden neighborhoods
were not at all more punitive than less fearful ones. At the
individual level, there were further difficulties with the argument: Women, who are much more fearful, are no more punitive; and blacks, who are somewhat more fearful, are a lot less
punitive.

   In Chapter Three we found the small relationship between
fear and punitiveness to be decreasing as fear becomes more
widespread, suggesting that high salience of a problem wipes
out social and ideological distinctions. In Chapter Four we

found that the relationship between liberalism and lenience stayed almost exactly the same during a period of increasing salience of crime, suggesting that social and ideological distinctions remain in spite of increased salience. In Chapter Six we found that in increasingly fearful neighborhoods, the association between liberalism and lenience increased, suggesting that increasing salience intensifies social and ideological distinctions and leads to polarization.

Much of the theorizing about the impact of strain on collective behavior argues that if the strain increases, then *something* will happen. For example, Smelser insists on adding six specifying variables before he is willing to predict specifically the form of the collective behavior (Smelser, 1962). Perhaps our demonstration that sometimes increased salience wipes out the association between punitive attitudes and social distinctions, sometimes leaves the association intact, and sometimes increases such correlations confirms the wisdom of social theory in not committing itself.

But let us ask what sort of effects should we generally expect from salience. Presumably an increase in the excitation level increases the intensity of whatever response was otherwise called for. That is, if the attribution or "definition" of the situation is not changed by the increased intensity or excitation, then the response should be the same as before but more intense or more frequent. Let us suppose, for example, that people living near black people in large central cities respond to all sorts of public policy questions principally by trying to figure out what to do about the ghetto. One solution comes from a liberal world view—more specifically from a notion that equality of treatment before the law through the courts is the last best hope and that the long-term remedy for ghetto problems consists in extending justice and busing. An alternative solution is to go in to the ghetto and "clean out the bad guys" so the rest of us can live in peace. Exactly who the bad guys are, who will clean them out, and who the rest of us are who will live in peace may not always be clear and may have racist overtones. If these alternative formulations of the problem are valid and if they are only found in neighborhoods near the ghetto, then an increase in the salience of crime would tend to polarize the population in those neighborhoods.

Suppose, for comparison, that in rural hunting America, there is no real organization of public policy questions regarding the ghetto. What is wrong with criminals is that they are bad, and they need to be punished. That is, the problem may be seen as in large measure an individualistic one. In this case, we would expect an increase in salience to result in an increase in measures directed at changing individuals, such as the threat of punishment. That is, increased salience of crime outside the big cities might cause increasing uniformity of punitiveness.

We argue, then, that our lack of understanding of the effects of salience is related to the attribution problem. What we do not understand about the effects of increased salience is supplied by the definition of the situation, which specifies the appropriate response for the increased salience: Fear can produce flight, aggression, quick nervous laughter, or voluble explanations, depending in part on whether one thinks that one can get away, that one can beat the enemy up, or that one can always talk one's way out of trouble. This argument implies that the effect of salience will almost always be an interaction effect: We have to know which kind of causal inference a strain is associated with before we can predict its outcome. Sometimes that inference will be a fixed and rigid response, obsessive or culturally traditional, and the effect of increased salience will be ritualistic. Sometimes the inference will be associated with uncertainty about whether it is right or not, and increased salience will result in increased research and learning. Sometimes increased salience will come in a context in which it calls up different world views in different parts of the population, and increased salience will result in polarization.

The general problem with interaction effects in social science is that it is hard to find multiple instances of variation in one of the variables with no variation of the values of the interacting variables. Specifically, there is no reason to suppose that variance over time in the salience of the crime problem between the middle 1960s and the middle 1970s is associated with the same kinds of variance by neighborhoods more or less exposed to the big city ghetto at a single point in time. We find that these two variations in the salience of crime (by time and by place) do not in fact have the same sorts of effects, and that variation between the races in the salience of crime has still another effect of exactly opposite sign from the over-time pattern. When we find that salience does not have the same effect on different races we are not surprised, but only because we know so much about why black people's judgments and causal assessments of court actions are likely to be different than those of white people. We need, but do not have, multiple theories of attribution to explain varying effects of salience.

To a large extent, this interaction effect of increased salience has been a disadvantage to the clarity of our argument; however, it also presents a great many research opportunities. Within any given group, we can explore the structure of associations of ideas by studying the impact of increases in salience. For example, if we want to find out as much as we can about the "natural tendencies" of black society on attitudes about crime and punishment, then we should arrange a study in which we can differentiate blacks by the salience of crime rather than classing all black people together and proceeding as if all of them lived in big city ghettos. Then we would find which causes of and remedies for crime are endorsed when crime is more salient and how these attitudes compare with those endorsed when crimes are more salient for whites.

Similarly, we could ask whether lenience more often becomes a part of a liberal world view in neighborhoods in which black people are more exposed to high rates of violent crime, as it does among whites. This requires us to obtain information about the structure of causal inference through which salience of crime is filtered in different American subcultures by observing the correlation of increased salience in those subcultures. Obviously, the more detailed information we have about our inferences about causes and remedies, the more we will learn by studying the increase in salience.

Applied or Basic Research?

This book is part research and part theoretical inquiry into public opinion. There is no continuous theoretical development from chapter to chapter in the elaboration of the findings, because there is a gap in social and psychological theory at the point at which the general public associates attitudes about solutions to public policy problems with increased worry about them. As we pointed out earlier, this gap raises important questions about the policy uses that are sometimes made of the trends in victimization, fear, and punitiveness summarized in Chapter Two. We believe that social theory should lend itself to practical application; we also believe that social indicator development requires rigorous and searching theoretical analyses such as those conducted in this study. We do not believe that we have filled the gap between public opinion and policy development in the area of crime control or in any other area. What we hope to have done is describe the nature of the gap as provocatively as possible, so that future research can more productively bridge it.

Appendix

Surveys Used and
Question Wordings

These questions have been used in many surveys other than
those listed here. This list includes only surveys used in this
book. SRS and General Social Surveys were conducted by the
National Opinion Research Center.

Topics	Wordings	Surveys	Year
Abortion —Liberalism	Please tell me whether or not *you* think it should be possible for a pregnant woman to obtain a *legal* abortion . . . A. If there is a strong chance of serious defect in the baby? B. If she is married and does not want any more children? C. If the woman's health is seriously endangered by the pregnancy?		

Topics	Wordings	Surveys	Year
	D. If the family has a very low income and cannot afford any more children?		
	E. If she became pregnant as a result of rape?		
	F. If she is not married and does not want to marry the man?	GSS74	1974
Busing	In general, do you favor or oppose the busing of (negro/black) and white school children from one school to another?		
		GSS72	1972
		GSS74	1974
		GSS75	1975
		GSS76	1976
		GSS77	1977
		GSS78	1978
Capital Punishment	Are you in favor of the death penalty for murder?		
		Gallup	1936
		Gallup 59	1936
		Gallup 105	1937
	Are you in favor of the death penalty for persons convicted of murder?		
		Gallup 522	1953
		Gallup 562	1956
		Gallup 588	1957
		Gallup 625	1960
		Gallup 704	1965
		Gallup 746	1967
		Gallup 774	1969
		Gallup 839	1971

Topics	Wordings	Surveys	Year
		Gallup 846	1972
		GSS72	1972
		Gallup 860	1972
		GSS73	1973
		Gallup 949	1976
	Do you think that having a death penalty for the worst crimes is a good idea, or are you against the death penalty?	SRS760	1964
	Do you favor or oppose the death penalty for persons convicted of murder?	GSS74	1974
		GSS75	1975
		GSS76	1976
		GSS77	1977
		GSS78	1978
Civil Liberties —Atheists	There are always some people whose ideas are considered bad or dangerous by other people. For instance, somebody who is against all churches and religion. A. If such a person wanted to make a speech in your community against churches and religion, should he be allowed to speak or not? B. Should such a person be allowed to teach in a college or university or not?		

Topics	Wordings	Surveys	Year
	C. If some people in your community suggested that a book he wrote against churches and religion should be taken out of your public library, would you favor removing this book or not?		
		GSS72	1972
		GSS74	1974
		GSS76	1976
		GSS77	1977
Civil Liberties —Communists	Now I should like to ask you some questions about a man who admits he is a Communist. A. Suppose this admitted Communist wanted to make a speech in your community. Should he be allowed to speak or not? B. Suppose he is teaching in a college. Should he be fired or not? C. Suppose he wrote a book which is in your public library. Somebody in your community suggests that the book should be removed from the library. Would		

Topics	Wordings	Surveys	Year
	you favor removing it or not?	GSS72	1972
		GSS74	1974
		GSS76	1976
		GSS77	1977
Civil Liberties —Homosexuals	And what about a man who admits that he is a homosexual?		
	A. Suppose this admitted homosexual wanted to make a speech in your community. Should he be allowed to speak or not?		
	B. Should such a person be allowed to teach in a college or university or not?		
	C. If some people in your community suggested that a book he wrote in favor of homosexuality should be taken out of your public library, would you favor removing this book or not?	GSS72	1972
		GSS74	1974
		GSS76	1976
		GSS77	1977
Civil Liberties —Socialists	Or consider a person who favored government ownership of all the railroads and all big industries.		

Topics	Wordings	Surveys	Year
	A. If such a person wanted to make a speech in your community favoring government ownership of all the railroads and big industries, should he be allowed to speak or not?		
	B. Should such a person be allowed to teach in a college or university or not?		
	C. If some people in your community suggested a book he wrote favoring government ownership should be taken out of your public library, would you favor removing this book or not?	GSS72	1972
		GSS74	1974
		GSS76	1976
		GSS77	1977
Courts	In general, do you think the courts in this area deal too harshly or not harshly enough with criminals?	Gallup 709	1965
		Gallup 716	1965
		Gallup 773	1969
		Gallup 861	1972
		GSS73	1973
		GSS74	1974
		GSS75	1975
		GSS76	1976
		GSS77	1977

Topics	Wordings	Surveys	Year
	In general, do you think the courts in this area deal too harshly, or not harshly enough with criminals, or don't you have enough information about the courts to say?	GSS74	1974
Fear	Is there any area right around here—that is, within a mile—where you would be afraid to walk alone at night?		
		Gallup 709	1965
		Gallup 749	1967
		Gallup 768	1968
		Gallup 847	1972
		Gallup 861	1972
		GSS73	1973
		GSS74	1974
		Gallup 93	1975
		GSS76	1976
		GSS77	1977
Feminism —Home	Do you agree or disagree with this statement? "Women should take care of running their homes and leave running the country up to men."	GSS74	1974
Feminism —Work	Do you approve or disapprove of a married woman earning money in business or industry if she has a husband capable of supporting her?	GSS74	1974

Topics	Wordings	Surveys	Year
Feminism —President	If your party nomin- ated a woman for president, would you vote for her if she were qualified for the job?	GSS74	1974
Feminism —Politics	Tell me if you agree or disagree with this statement: "Most men are better suited emotionally for politics than are most women."	GSS74	1974
	Would you say that most men are better suited for politics than are most women, that men and women are equally suited, or that women are better suited than men in this area?	GSS74	1974
Gun Control —Police Permit	Would you favor or oppose a law which would require a person to obtain a police permit before he or she could buy a gun?	Gallup 616	1959
		Gallup 681	1963
		Gallup 704	1965
		Gallup 717	1966
		Gallup 749	1967
		Gallup 838	1971
		Gallup 852	1972
		GSS72	1972
		GSS73	1973
		GSS74	1974
		GSS75	1975

Topics	Wordings	Surveys	Year
Gun Control —Registration	Do you favor or oppose federal laws which would control the sales of guns, such as making all persons register all gun purchases no matter where they buy them?	Harris Harris	1968 1975
Gun Ownership and Type	Do you happen to have in your home any guns or revolvers; *IF YES:* Is it a pistol, shotgun, rifle, or what?	Gallup 852 Gallup 704 Gallup 733	1959 1965 1966
	Do you happen to have in your home (IF HOUSE: or garage) any guns or revolvers? *IF YES:* Is it a pistol, shotgun, rifle, or what?	Gallup 852 GSS73 GSS74 GSS76 GSS77	1972 1973 1974 1976 1977
Hunters	Do you or your (husband/wife) hunt?	Gallup 616 Gallup 704 Gallup 733	1959 1965 1966
Liberalism —Self-description	We hear a lot of talk these days about liberals and conservatives. I'm going to show you a seven-point scale on which the *political* views that people might hold are arranged		

Topics	Wordings	Surveys	Year
	from extremely liberal –point 1–to extremely conservative–point 7. Where would you place yourself on this scale? 1. Extremely liberal 2. Liberal 3. Slightly liberal 4. Moderate, middle of the road 5. Slightly conservative 6. Conservative 7. Extremely conservative	GSS74 GSS75 GSS76	1974 1975 1976
Most Important Problem	What do you think is the most important problem facing this country today? (This is the standard version of the question. The data in Table 3 come from about seventy Gallup surveys conducted during the years listed. Eleven other wordings were also used. For a list of these other wordings, see Smith 1976a).		1946 1947 1948 1949 1950 1951 1954 1955 1956 1957 1958 1959 1960 1962 1963 1964 1965 1966 1967

Topics	Wordings	Surveys	Year
			1968
			1969
			1970
			1971
			1972
			1973
Neighborhood Integration	Are there any (negroes/ blacks) living in this neighborhood now?	GSS72	1972
		GSS73	1973
		GSS74	1974
		GSS75	1975
		GSS76	1976
Racial Prejudice —Dinner (attitude)	How strongly would you object if a member of your family wanted to bring a (negro/black) friend home to dinner? Would you object strongly, mildly, or not at all?	GSS73	1973
		GSS74	1974
		GSS76	1976
		GSS77	1977
Racial Prejudice —Dinner (behavior)	During the last few years, has anyone in your family brought a friend who was a (negro/black) home for dinner?	GSS73	1973
		GSS74	1974
		GSS76	1976
		GSS77	1977
Racial Prejudice —Intermarriage	Do you think there should be laws against marriages between (negroes/blacks) and whites?	SRS760	1964
		GSS72	1972

Topics	Wordings	Surveys	Year
		GSS73	1973
		GSS74	1974
		GSS75	1975
		GSS76	1976
		GSS77	1977
		GSS78	1978
Racial Prejudice —School Integration	Do you think white students and (negro/ black) students should go to the same schools or to separate schools?	SRS760	1964
		GSS72	1972
		GSS76	1976
		GSS77	1977
Sexual Liberalism —Information for teenagers	Do you think birth control *information* should be available to teenagers who want it or not?	GSS74	1974
Sexual Liberalism —Sex Education	Would you be for or against sex education in the public schools?	GSS74	1974
Sexual Liberalism —Divorce	Should divorce in this country be easier or more difficult to obtain than it is now?	GSS74	1974
Sexual Liberalism —Premarital sex	There's been a lot of discussion about the way morals and attitudes about sex are changing in this country. If a man and a woman have sex relations before marriage, do you think it is always wrong, almost always		

Topics	Wordings	Surveys	Year
	wrong, wrong only sometimes, or not wrong at all?	GSS74	1974
Sexual Liberalism —Homo- sexuality	What about sexual re- lations between two adults of the same sex—do you think it is always wrong, almost always wrong, wrong only sometimes, or not wrong at all?	GSS74	1974
Victimization —Burglary	During the last year— that is, between March and now— did anyone break into or somehow illegally get into your (apartment/home)?	GSS73 GSS74	1973 1974
Victimization —Robbery	During the last year, did anyone take something directly from you by using force—such as a stickup, mugging, or threat?	GSS73 GSS74 GSS76 GSS77	1973 1974 1976 1977

References

Achen, C. H. "Mass Political Attitudes and the Survey Response." *American Political Science Review,* 1975, *69,* 1218-1231.

Amir, M. *Patterns in Forcible Rape.* Chicago: University of Chicago Press, 1971.

Biderman, A. D., and others. *Report on a Pilot Study in the District of Columbia on Victimization and Attitudes Toward Law Enforcement.* U.S. President's Committee on Law Enforcement and the Administration of Justice Field Survey I. Washington, D.C.: U.S. Government Printing Office, 1967.

Burke, K. *A Grammar of Motive.* Berkeley: University of California Press, 1969.

Conklin, J. E. "Dimensions of Community Response to the Crime Problem." *Social Problems,* 1971, *18,* 375-385.

Converse, P. E. "The Nature of Belief Systems in Mass Publics." In D. Apter (Ed.), *Ideology and Discontent.* New York: Free Press, 1964.

162

Converse, P. E. "Attitudes and Nonattitudes: Continuation of a Dialogue." In E. R. Tufte (Ed.), *The Quantitative Analysis of Social Problems.* Reading, Mass.: Addison-Wesley, 1970.

Curtis, L. A. *Criminal Violence.* Lexington, Mass.: Heath, 1974.

Davis, F. J. "Crime News in Colorado Newspapers." *American Journal of Sociology,* 1952, *57,* 325-350.

Davis, J. A. "Communism, Conformity, Cohorts, and Categories." *American Journal of Sociology,* 1975, *81,* 491-513.

Durkheim, E. *The Division of Labor in Society.* (G. Simpson, Trans.) New York: Free Press, 1964. (Originally published 1893.)

Erbe, B. M. "On 'The Politics of School Busing.' " *Public Opinion* Quarterly, 1977, *41,* 113-117.

Evers, M., and McGee, J. "The Trend and Pattern in Attitudes Toward Abortion: 1965-1976." Paper presented at the Annual Meeting of the American Sociological Association, Chicago, August 1977.

Federal Bureau of Investigation. *Uniform Crime Reports for the United States.* Washington, D.C.: United States Government Printing Office, 1960-1978.

Field, J. O., and Anderson, R. E. "Ideology in the Public's Conceptualization of the 1964 Election." *Public Opinion Quarterly,* 1969, *33,* 380-398.

Furstenberg, F. F. "Public Reaction to Crime in the Streets." *The American Scholar,* 1971, *40,* 601-610.

Heberle, R. *Social Movements.* New York: Appleton-Century-Crofts, 1951.

Heise, D. "Affective Dynamics in Simple Sentences." *Journal of Personality and Social Psychology,* 1969, *11,* 204-213.

Heise, D. "Social Action as the Control of Affect." *Behavioral Science,* 1977, *22,* 163-177.

Hindelang, M. J. *Criminal Victimization in Eight American Cities.* Cambridge, Mass.: Ballinger, 1976.

Kadish, S. N. "The Crisis of Overcriminalization." *Annals of the American Academy of Political and Social Science,* 1967, *374,* 157-170.

Kelley, J. "The Politics of School Busing." *Public Opinion Quarterly,* 1974, *38,* 23-39.

Kennett, L., and Anderson, J. L. *The Gun in America: The Origins of a National Dilemma.* Westport, Conn.: Greenwood Press, 1975.

Land, K., and Felson, M. "A General Framework for Modeling Dynamic Macro Social Indicator Models: Including an Analysis of Changes in Crime Rates and Police Expenditures." *American Journal of Sociology,* 1976, *82,* 565-604.

McClosky, R. G. "The American Ideology." In M. D. Irish (Ed.), *Continuing Crisis in American Politics.* Englewood Cliffs, N.J.: Prentice-Hall, 1963.

McIntyre, J. "Public Attitudes Toward Crime and Law Enforcement." *Annals of the American Academy of Political and Social Science,* 1967, *374,* 34-46.

Margolis, M. "From Confusion to Confusion: Issues and the American Voter (1956-1972)." *American Political Science Review,* 1977, *71,* 31-43.

Myrdal, G. *An American Dilemma.* New York: Harper & Row, 1962.

Newton, G. D., and Zimring, F. E. *Firearms and Violence in American Life.* Washington, D.C.: U.S. Government Printing Office, 1969.

Nie, N., Verba, S., and Petrocik, J. R. *The Changing American Voter.* Cambridge, Mass.: Harvard University Press, 1976.

Office of Management and the Budget, Statistical Policy Division. *Social Indicators: 1973.* Washington, D.C.: U.S. Government Printing Office, 1973.

Pierce, J. C., and Rose, D. D. "Nonattitudes and American Public Opinion: The Examination of a Thesis." *American Political Science Review,* 1974, *68,* 626-649.

President's Commission on Law Enforcement and the Administration of Justice. *The Challenge of Crime in a Free Society.* Washington, D.C.: U.S. Government Printing Office, 1967.

Reader's Guide to Periodical Literature. New York: H. W. Wilsen, 1930-1978.

Rosett, A. "The Negotiated Guilty Plea." *Annals of the American Academy of Political and Social Science,* 1967, *374,* 70-81.

Shaw, C., and McKay, H. *Delinquency Areas.* Chicago: University of Chicago Press, 1942.

Smelser, N. J. *The Theory of Collective Behavior.* London: Routledge and Kegan Paul, 1962.

Smith, T. W. "America's Most Important Problem: A Trend Analysis, 1946-1976." Paper presented to the Midwest Association for Public Opinion Research, October 1976a.

Smith, T. W. "A Study of Trends in the Political Role of Women." In J. A. Davis (Ed.), *Studies of Social Change Since 1948.* National Opinion Research Center, Report 127B. Chicago: National Opinion Research Center, 1976b.

Smith, T. W. "A Trend Analysis of Attitudes Toward Capital Punishment, 1936-1974." In J. A. Davis (Ed.), *Studies of Social Change Since 1948.* National Opinion Research Center, Report 127B. Chicago: National Opinion Research Center, 1976c.

Smith, T. W. "Crime Counting: A Discussion of the Reliability of the Uniform Crime Reports' (UCR) Accounting of Crime." Unpublished manuscript, National Opinion Research Center, 1977.

Stinchcombe, A. L., and Taylor, D. G. "On Democracy and School Integration." In J. Feagin and W. Stephan (Eds.), *Desegregation: Past, Present, and Future.* New York: Plenum, 1980.

Taylor, D. G. "The Diffusion and Change of Public Attitudes Toward Some Social Issues in Recent American History." Unpublished doctoral dissertation, University of Chicago, 1977.

Taylor, D. G. "Housing, Neighborhoods, and Race Relations: Recent Survey Evidence." *Annals of the American Academy of Political and Social Science,* 1979, *441,* 26-40.

Taylor, D. G. "Procedures for Evaluating Trends in Public Opinion." *Public Opinion Quarterly,* 1980, *44,* 86-100.

Taylor, D. G., Scheppele, K., and Stinchcombe, A. L. "Salience of Crime and Support for Harsher Criminal Sanctions." *Social Problems,* 1979, *26,* 413-424.

Taylor, D. G., Sheatsley, P. B., and Greeley, A. M. "Attitudes Toward Racial Integration." *Scientific American,* 1978, *238,* 42-49.

Tocqueville, A. de. *Democracy in America.* (H. Reeve, Trans.) New York: Vintage, 1945. (Originally published 1848.)

U.S. Bureau of the Census. *Statistical Abstract of the United States: 1972.* Washington, D.C.: U.S. Government Printing Office, 1972.

U.S. Bureau of the Census. *Historical Statistics of the United States, Colonial Times to 1970.* Bicentennial Edition, Part 2. Washington, D.C.: U.S. Government Printing Office, 1975.

U.S. Bureau of the Census. *Statistical Abstract of the United States: 1976.* Washington, D.C.: U.S. Government Printing Office, 1976.

U.S. Congress, House, Committee on the Judiciary, Subcommittee on Crime, 94th Congress, 1st Session. *Firearms Legislation.* Washington, D.C.: U.S. Government Printing Office, 1975.

von Hentig, H. *The Criminal and His Victim.* New Haven, Conn.: Yale University Press, 1948.

Wilks, J. "Ecological Correlates of Crime and Delinquency." Appendix A of *Crime and Its Impact: An Assessment.* Report of President's Commission on Law Enforcement and Administration of Justice. Washington, D.C.: U.S. Government Printing Office, 1967.

Williams, B. "Democracy and Ideology." *Political Quarterly,* 1961, *32,* 374-384.

Wolfgang, M. E. *Patterns in Criminal Homicide.* New York: Wiley, 1958.

Wolfgang, M. E., and Cohen, B. *Crime and Race.* New York: Institute of Human Relations Press, 1970.

Zimring, F. E., and Hawkins, G. *Deterrence: The Legal Threat in Crime Control.* Chicago: University of Chicago Press, 1973.

Index